FALLEN IDOLS

© Haynes Publishing, 2013

The right of Carol King to be identified as the author of this Work has been asserted by her in accordance with the Copyright, Designs & Patents Act 1988.

First published in 2013

A catalogue record for this book is available from the British Library

ISBN: 978-0-85733-208-0

Published by Haynes Publishing, Sparkford, Yeovil,
Somerset BA22 7JJ, UK
Tel: 01963 442030 Fax: 01963 440001
Int. tel: +44 1963 442030 Int. fax: +44 1963 440001
E-mail: sales@haynes.co.uk
Website: www.haynes.co.uk

Haynes North America Inc., 861 Lawrence Drive, Newbury Park, California 91320, USA

Images © Mirrorpix

Creative Director: Kevin Gardner
Designed for Haynes by BrainWave

Printed and bound in the US

F LLEN IDOLS

Carol King

FALLEN IDOLS

CONTENTS

INTRODUCTION:
THE PRICE OF FAME
6

CHAPTER ONE:
BURNED TRAILBLAZERS
8

CHAPTER TWO:
A SHOCK TO THE NATION
25

CHAPTER THREE:
LADY LUCK TURNS SOUR
72

CHAPTER FOUR:
A TASTE FOR EXCESS
116

CHAPTER FIVE:
NOTORIOUS NIGHTMARES
175

INTRODUCTION:

THE PRICE OF FAME

Success. Fame. Adulation. Wealth. Power. And then?

Fallen Idols charts the fall from grace of iconic figures in the public eye. Some bounced back, while others didn't. Some were hailed as heroes and icons until they died, and it was only afterwards their dirty secrets came to light. Ironically, others were the focus of negative attention while they were alive, and were then rehabilitated in the public consciousness after their deaths.

Politicians, actors, business gurus, athletes and musicians gain attention because of their skill – royals and aristocracy because of their privilege. Their success can inspire others, their good deeds can change lives for the better. Their stories of hard work, sometimes a lucky break, combined with dedication, ambition and drive can seem like fairytales. Carefully crafted interviews, well-chosen appearances, artfully lit photo shoots, airbrushed photographs and the workings of the publicity machine contribute to creating an image. But the individuals behind the artful public image may be very different and only really known by those closest to them. Unsurprisingly, the public can be shocked when the famous falter and perhaps even disappoint – since they appeared to have it all, why did they throw it away?

The answer remains elusive. In some cases, it appears that the pressure of life led in the glare of publicity was intolerable. For others, a love of success and its ensuing benefits meant they did everything they could to hold on to it, sometimes crossing the line to do so. Others hid behind their fame, using the power it gave them to conceal nefarious activities.

Society chooses to idolize those who sing songs, create a character on celluloid, kick a ball, have entrepreneurial chutzpah, look attractive and appear on podia to make speeches. Our blind admiration does them a disservice; we forget they are only people, not gods. They represent the best and worst of us, possessing all the foibles and frailties, virtues and vices that come with being human. Their misadventures just happen to be recorded. They are a lesson that money, power and fame do not always bring happiness, and that the great are not necessarily good.

In the 21st century, thanks to the Internet, news spreads faster than ever across the globe. Social media is lightning fast at disseminating both fact and hearsay. Armed with digital devices, the public snaps pictures as much as the paparazzi. It has never been so hard for an idol not to fall.

CHAPTER ONE:

BURNED TRAILBLAZERS

Silent films gave the world its first global icons. Their silence was key because, by slotting in written translations, they could be watched anywhere in the world. The films catapulted their stars to fame: vaudeville artist Charlie Chaplin stepped in front of a film camera for the first time in January 1914 and by the end of the year he was the most widely recognized person on the planet. By the 1920s, Hollywood was the centre of the film industry. The star system was in place and cinemagoers read about their favourite actors and actresses in newspapers and fan magazines like *Photoplay*. Celebrities were born, and with them came a flood of gossip about their lives off-screen. Stars lived lavish lifestyles, giving credence to the idea that, in America, anyone could be a success; they typified a glamorous notion of the American Dream. However, not everyone was won over by films: some parts of society regarded them as a negative influence because they portrayed crime, violence and sexual openness. Hollywood and its stars came to represent the so-called "New Morality" of sexual freedom, autonomy for women and consumerism that for some reeked of dark hedonism, sexual immorality and extravagance.

In 1921, American slapstick comic and director Roscoe "Fatty" Arbuckle was Hollywood's highest-paid actor. The star of Keystone Kops, Arbuckle was a friend and mentor of Chaplin and Buster Keaton. Arbuckle was Tinseltown's darling until he was arrested for the rape and murder of 26-year-old starlet Virginia Rappe. It was Hollywood's first big scandal.

On 5th September 1921, Labor Day, 34-year-old Arbuckle threw a wild party at the St Francis Hotel in San Francisco to celebrate a million-dollar studio deal. It was the Prohibition era when alcohol was banned, yet everybody was pretty drunk on bootleg booze when 20-stone Arbuckle took Rappe into his bedroom at the hotel. The door was locked, and witnesses later told of strange moans and piercing screams. When Arbuckle reappeared in sweat-soaked pyjamas with Rappe's hat perched on his head he wheezed: "Take her away she makes too much noise."

In the bedroom, the half-naked Rappe moaned: "I'm dying! I'm dying!"

Two days later, Rappe was hospitalized. She died on 9th September, having told a startled nurse: "Fatty Arbuckle did this to me. Make sure he doesn't get away with it."

A suspicious state coroner investigated Rappe's death and arrived at a post-mortem just in time to stop a hospital orderly burning the actress' injured female organs. A companion of Rappe's at the party, Bambina Maude Delmont, told the police that Arbuckle raped Rappe.

The post-mortem revealed bruises on Rappe's body but no evidence of rape. There were stories that Arbuckle, enraged by drunken impotence, had tried to ravage Rappe by repeatedly jumping on her, and that his weight had caused the damage. Delmont accused Arbuckle of murder and he was arrested.

At the coroner's inquest, Delmont stated that Arbuckle dragged Rappe into a bedroom and locked the door, and she heard screams coming from the bedroom an hour afterwards. Delmont added that when Arbuckle finally opened the door at her request, she found Rappe lying on the bed, tearing at her clothing and screaming: "I'm dying! I'm dying! He did it!"

Delmont testified that she drank 10 glasses of whisky at the party. When the coroner asked her how she could remember what had happened, she replied: "My memory is always good."

She said that Rappe did not drink any whisky, but had three glasses of gin mixed with wine in Arbuckle's apartment. Two other witnesses, Zey Prevost and Alice Blake, told the same story about Rappe screaming. Asked if Arbuckle had talked much, Prevost said: "Yes, he was very wroth. I asked him what he was mad about. He replied: 'If she makes one more yell I will throw her out of the window.'"

Prevost said that Arbuckle was intoxicated. He had been talking about jumping out of a 12th-storey window, saying: "What is life, after all?"

Both Prevost and Blake requested to be placed in the care of a policewoman to prevent any chance of intimidation. Rappe's manager, Al Semnacher, testified that when he visited Rappe the next day she told him that Arbuckle had injured her. Nurse Jean Jameson, whose affidavit was the primary cause for the charge of murder against Arbuckle, testified that before Rappe died the starlet told her that she did not know whether she had been assaulted or not. The concluding witness at the inquest was a police detective who testified to examining the hotel room where the attack was alleged to have taken place, and to finding the toe marks of a woman's shoe on several places on the wall. Arbuckle appeared indifferent to everything in the courtroom, paying no attention to the photographers who were snapping him from every angle, and disdaining to reply to the questions of would-be interviewers. His lawyers declared that the evidence presented ensured his acquittal.

The inquest concluded that Rappe died of peritonitis, caused by a ruptured bladder and brought about by "external pressure". The coroner's jury found Arbuckle guilty of manslaughter. The jury added a rider recommending the authorities take steps "to prevent the further occurrence of such events, so that San Francisco shall not be made the rendezvous of gangs of debauchees". Although apparently deeply moved, Arbuckle accepted the verdict with composure. He was arraigned to appear before a grand jury on a charge of murder.

Arbuckle, the cuddly clown so loved by America's children, was involved in a gruesome tale. Within a week of Rappe's death, Arbuckle went from a Hollywood idol to the most decried figure in American public life. Sales of newspapers soared as they recounted prurient details of the squalid story in sensational terms. The day the verdict was announced, a group of cowboys invaded the Maverick Theatre in Thermopolis, Wyoming, where an Arbuckle film was being shown. They riddled the screen with bullets, and then carried the film reel into the street and burned it. The public's aversion for Arbuckle was not confined to America: even as far away as Melbourne in Australia his films were withdrawn, pending the outcome of the case.

It was not only the evidence presented that aroused public indignation: people were shocked by the revelations of wild orgies organized by the Hollywood film community. A number of women's clubs, co-operating with the churches of Los Angeles, had succeeded in smuggling witnesses into the studios and other places where the purported orgies were held. The witnesses went on to recite lurid stories, disclosing decadence in the film community.

Yet Arbuckle's estranged wife, Minta Durfee, rushed to defend him, saying: "He is nothing but a loveable, overgrown schoolboy. He cannot be guilty of so terrible a crime. He is full of fun, and that he should think of stooping to what is nothing but a most serious crime is unthinkable. I mean to stay by him all through this. All our differences are forgotten in face of this terrible event, with all its possibilities." Durfee kept her word. She stood by her husband throughout the ordeal, and frequently attended court to show her support for him.

Hours before the grand jury convened, Semnacher told the press that Arbuckle had inserted a piece of ice into Rappe's vagina in an apparent sex game. The newspapers were full of headlines that Arbuckle had tortured the starlet – and in some reports the ice had transformed by exaggeration into a bottle. However, when Semnacher testified at the hearing, his story changed. He said that the partygoers had sat around in pyjamas drinking gin and whisky while a phonograph played, and that the morning after the party Arbuckle had described his "prank" of administering ice to Rappe. Semnacher had not witnessed the purported incident and three other witnesses had already testified that Arbuckle had placed ice on Rappe's stomach thinking she had a stomach ache.

Then the defence went on the attack, accusing Semnacher of conspiring with Delmont to take portions of Rappe's clothing to Los Angeles for the purpose of extorting money from Arbuckle. Semnacher denied the accusation and threatened to sue Arbuckle's attorney for defamation of character. Prevost testified that Rappe had been given a restorative and was then dipped in a tub of cold water. Prevost revealed that someone then telephoned for aid, but another guest jerked away the receiver, explaining he did not want notoriety.

However, the state prosecutor, Matthew Brady, chose not to put Arbuckle's principal accuser, Delmont, on the witness stand. The defence complained, wanting to have the opportunity to approve that her accusations were "falsehoods", but she could not be compelled to appear. Brady baulked at putting Delmont on the stand because his star witness was known as a bigamist and blackmailer, and suspected of being involved in prostitution and swindling. The judge was surprised at the paucity of evidence presented by the ambitious Brady for the prosecution and warned him that he was in danger of having the case dismissed because of lack of proof. He also refused to entertain the suggestion of murder, saying that the evidence produced was insufficient, but that Arbuckle would have to face a charge of manslaughter. The judge said: "In a sense we are trying ourselves, our morals and present-day social standards, a question larger than the guilt of this defendant."

After 18 days in jail, Arbuckle was let out on bail of $5,000. As the court adjourned, a dozen women rushed forward to shake Arbuckle's hand. The comedian – his face wreathed in smiles and with a bundle of clothing under his arm – was accompanied by his wife. They proceeded to the judge's chambers, where she collapsed. Arbuckle held her up and quieted her down in an affectionate manner. Only days later, Arbuckle was arrested for an alleged violation of the Prohibition law concerning the alcohol served in his hotel suite. He pleaded guilty and paid a $500 fine.

Three sensational trials followed. The first began on 14th November in San Francisco, and a huge crowd gathered outside the court building in the hope they might get in, despite the fact that the authorities had issued a notice saying no more than 300 people could be admitted. Arbuckle appeared worried and looked nervously around the packed court.

The defence said its case would be based on physiological questions, contending that at the time of Rappe's death she was suffering from chronic cystitis that flared up when she drank and which had been diagnosed at least eight years earlier. On the first day of the trial, the defence cast doubt on the veracity of the witnesses' statements, when Arbuckle's lead counsel told the court that he had evidence to prove that witnesses had been taken to the city prison and intimidated by the district attorney to testify against the comedian. His team of lawyers also attempted to prove that he had not spent more than 10 minutes alone in the room with Rappe. A maid at the hotel gave evidence that she had dusted the doors, previously mentioned in the case as having borne Rappe and Arbuckle's fingerprints. The defence endeavoured to prove that the maid had wiped off any fingerprints.

Film director Fred Fischbach, who, along with Arbuckle, occupied the hotel suite where the tragedy occurred, said he had found Rappe in a hysterical condition on the bed in the room and assisted in putting her into the bath. Fischbach told the court that Rappe did not appear to be in pain but "seemed suffering from the effects of alcohol". On 3rd December, the jury was dismissed because it failed to reach a verdict.

The second trial began on 11th January 1922, with the same judge, legal defence and prosecution. However, Prevost testified that the district attorney, Brady, had forced her to lie. Another witness was outed as an ex-convict and had testified in exchange for Brady reducing a sentence on an assault charge. Rappe was revealed as a heavy drinker. One of Rappe's nurses, Irene Morgan, had disappeared and could not give evidence. The defence argued that she had left the country and that had been arranged after the first trial. Even more bizarrely, after Morgan gave evidence at the first trial she had eaten some poisoned sweets given to her by a man on the street. Later, she was found unconscious but managed to recover. At the first trial, a criminologist, Dr Edward Heinrich, had suggested that Arbuckle's fingerprints were superimposed over those of Rappe on the bathroom door of the hotel suite, suggesting the two had struggled while she attempted to close the door. In the second trial, Heinrich changed his mind and said that he believed the fingerprint evidence had been faked.

The prosecution's case fell apart. Arbuckle's lawyers were so convinced that he would be acquitted they did not call on him to testify. However, some of the jurors took the defence's refusal to let Arbuckle take the stand as an admission of guilt. The jury was deadlocked and a mistrial was declared.

Arbuckle's third trial began on 13th March. This time, he testified. The jury took six minutes to acquit him on the charge of manslaughter. The speed of the verdict was unexpected and Arbuckle received it with a sigh of relief. His wife wept. After the adjournment of the court, the jury foreman read a statement: "Acquittal is not enough for Roscoe Arbuckle. We feel that a great injustice has been done to him … there was not the slightest proof adduced to connect him in any way with the commission of a crime. He was manly throughout the case and told a straightforward story which we all believe. We wish him success and hope that the American people will take the judgement of fourteen men and women that Roscoe Arbuckle is entirely innocent and free from all blame."

Arbuckle was innocent. Nevertheless, Rappe had her way. His life was ruined. He sold his house and cars to pay his legal fees. In 1924, Durfee divorced him. Arbuckle remarried a year later, to actress Doris Deane. However, Arbuckle took to drinking to drown his sorrows and the marriage ended in divorce after five years. The damage to Arbuckle's acting career was permanent. The American Women's Club forced Arbuckle out of pictures: his film contract was cancelled and his reputation was in shreds. He tried in vain to stage a comeback, aided by friends, but his films were banned from American screens. When he went to Paris as a music-hall artist, he did not win favour. In 1928, Arbuckle became the proprietor of the Plantation Café nightclub in Culver City, Los Angeles. On opening night Hollywood attended in full force, and Arbuckle performed for his peers, including Charlie Chaplin, Buster Keaton, Mary Pickford and Douglas

Fairbanks. But the stock market crash of October 1929 proved bad for business and Arbuckle had to close the club.

Although unable to return to the screen, Arbuckle did manage to find work directing comedies under the pseudonym "William Goodrich". In 1924, Arbuckle's protégée Keaton asked him to direct his latest comedy, *Sherlock Jr*. However, Keaton had to remove Arbuckle after only a few days because the stress of the trials had made him a nervous wreck and working with him was impossible. Nevertheless, Keaton used his influence to persuade Marion Davies, girlfriend of newspaper magnate William Randolph Hearst, to use Arbuckle as director on 1927's *The Red Mill*, starring Davies. Hearst's production company, Cosmopolitan Pictures, produced the film – the newspaper tycoon is said to have felt guilty about helping to destroy Arbuckle's career because his newspapers attacked the star after his arrest. Arbuckle went on to direct films under the guise of William Goodrich until 1932.

The former screen idol was almost forgotten by the public until 1932, when Arbuckle suddenly announced his engagement to stage actress Addie McPhail. The couple married later that year. At the same time, influential people in the film industry tried to persuade Hollywood to pardon the dethroned comedian, and it was felt that his return to the screen would prove a box-office attraction. In 1932, Warner Bros offered Arbuckle a second chance, with a comeback contract to star in two shorts. He finished the films on 28th June 1933. The next day, Warner Bros signed him to make a feature. In a cruel twist of fate, 46-year-old Arbuckle died of a heart attack in his sleep at his New York hotel apartment that same night.

It has been suggested that Arbuckle was railroaded on phoney charges pressed by anti-Hollywood politicians and churchmen. The truth of what happened that night is unknown. Initially, Delmont claimed she was a lifelong friend of Rappe's; however, the reality was that she had only met Rappe a few days before the ill-fated party at the hotel. Some have speculated that Delmont concocted a story to gain fame and money. Others posit she was in league with Semnacher to extort money from Arbuckle. Whatever the truth, Delmont was an unreliable witness.

Arbuckle claimed that he had found Rappe vomiting in the hotel bathroom and had taken her to the bedroom because she was ill. Rappe had a reputation for getting drunk, which exacerbated her chronic illness. She then tore at her clothes from the pain and distress caused by drinking suspect bootleg booze. Some have speculated that Rappe had had a botched abortion, which accounted for her pain and subsequent death. There have also been suggestions that, in the horseplay atmosphere of the party, Arbuckle attempted to calm her down by putting some ice on her body but banged into her, causing pain in her perhaps already damaged internal organs.

The district attorney's insistence on prosecuting the case against Arbuckle despite a lack of evidence – perhaps to gain publicity and advance his own career – propelled news of the incident on to front pages worldwide. The inconsistency of witness statements and accusations of shady deals done by the prosecution to bolster the case makes reviewing it decades afterwards difficult. Nevertheless, some have tried. In 2011, British presenter and comedian Paul Merton attempted to right what he saw as unfair wrong against the silent-film hero in his BBC documentary series *Paul Merton's Birth of Hollywood*. Merton re-enacted the night of that fateful party to prove that the real scandal was not what Arbuckle did, but how outrageously trumped up the charges against him were.

Arbuckle was found innocent of murder. However, some at the time regarded the mere fact he threw a party, invited women and drank alcohol as symptomatic of the worst excesses of Hollywood. Arbuckle was made to suffer for Hollywood's perceived decadence in a signal to the film industry that no one was so famous that they could not be brought down by the climate of public opinion. Hollywood sacrificed the comic genius to ensure its survival.

Another of Hollywood's first idols also fell from her pedestal thanks to a court case: the "flaming-haired film star", American actress Clara Bow. She brought aggressive sex appeal to the silent films of the Roaring Twenties, and later talkies, by playing the independent-minded, working-class flapper. Millions flocked to see the screen's first sex symbol and thousands of them were shocked. In the late 1920s and early 1930s, her name was one for the gossip sheets.

Bow came to fame in films like the 1926 comedy *Mantrap*, in which she played a flirtatious manicurist, and in the first film to ever win an Academy Award for Best Picture, 1927's *Wings*, in which she played an ambulance driver. She was society's first-ever "It Girl" thanks to her starring role as a spirited shop assistant in the 1927 romantic comedy silent *It*. Bow had the sexy looks, provocative glance and sassy attitude required to give the audience what they wanted. She once said: "I've always played sexy roles, put my hand on my hips and rolled my eyes."

Off-screen, her love life was notorious. She became known for her affair with actor Gary Cooper and "publicity engagements" to director Victor Fleming, actor Gilbert Roland and actor Harry Richman. Her relationship with a married doctor, Earl Pearson, led to his wife suing her for "alienation of affection" in a divorce case. Bow said later: "The wife sued me for 150,000 smackers. Blam! Just like that! I've never seen that much money."

Yet the cinemagoing public continued to love the non-conformist Bow. Her fall began when she sacked her secretary, Daisy DeVoe, in November 1930. The following month, DeVoe was arrested for stealing from the film star. Initially, Bow was unwilling to appear in court against her and the investigation was postponed. Nevertheless, DeVoe was charged with having stolen $30,000 in cash, clothing and jewellery from her employer. A trial ensued.

The trial began on 13th January 1931 at Los Angeles County Courthouse, and the story was reported around the world. DeVoe's stories of her former employer's affairs, drinking and gambling painted a picture of a promiscuous woman. Bow found DeVoe's mudslinging accusations intolerable and there was a dramatic scene when Bow gave evidence. Having caught DeVoe's gaze fixed on her, she screamed out in court: "All right. Go ahead. Sneer at me, Daisy."

DeVoe merely turned her face away, but Bow, putting her handkerchief over her eyes, began to weep. The courtroom was littered with fur coats, silk dresses and other finery alleged to have been purchased by DeVoe. In February, DeVoe was convicted on a charge of embezzlement and sentenced to five years probation, of which the first 18 months were to be spent in jail.

The publicity surrounding Bow's trial ruined her reputation. She may have been the accuser and victim, but her lifestyle had gone on trial and the public were shocked. Worse was to come. In April, the editor of the *Coast Reporter* newspaper that dealt with titbits of scandal, Frederic Girnau, was arrested on a charge of circulating obscene matter through the mail. The material in question was an article titled "The Life of Clara Bow", serialized over three weeks. It claimed to be based on alleged affidavits made by DeVoe, although she denied it. Bow's father informed the authorities of a "plot" against his daughter that included a $25,000 blackmail demand as the purchase price of the scurrilous paper.

The sleazy tabloid's outrageous claims were so sensational as to be almost laughable. The *Coast Reporter* claimed Bow slept with men, women and even animals, in the form of her pet koala and Great Dane. She was said to have committed incest by seducing her cousin Billy. The paper claimed Bow was a promiscuous exhibitionist: she was mistress to several men and had indulged in a threesome with prostitutes. On top of this, the scandal sheet asserted she was an alcoholic, a drug addict and had contracted sexually transmitted diseases. Girnau was jailed for what was branded one of the most vicious attacks ever printed in a paper – while the rumours that the article started swirled around Hollywood and beyond.

The situation took its toll on Bow. She was reluctant to face another court case and, having sometimes worked on three films at once, was exhausted from years of overwork. Girnau's slander was the last straw. In early May, Bow was taken to a Hollywood sanatorium following a "nervous collapse" in a studio, and her condition was reported to be serious. Redhead Peggy Shannon replaced Bow in her latest film, *The Secret Call*, while the star spent time in a nursing home suffering from "shattered nerves". Then Bow parted company with her studio, Paramount Famous Lasky Corporation. It appeared that DeVoe's revelations about Bow's life had damaged both the star and her career.

In June, Bow left Hollywood to spend time recovering from her nervous breakdown with her fiancé, actor Rex Bell, on his ranch in Nevada. By October, Shannon was already touted as Bow's successor. However, Bow's adoring fans did not forget her: during her absence from the screen she received more than 200,000 letters from people anxious to know when she would make her next appearance. In December, Bow married Bell in a secret ceremony in Nevada. The same month, it was announced that Bow had signed up with Columbia Pictures and had started work on another film. The film never happened.

Bow's stressful experience and subsequent illness had changed her. In January 1932, Hollywood newspaper reporters had the shock of their lives when Bow returned to work. They were all ready for her to give them a front-page story as she had always done in the past. However, Bow had learned that too much publicity is harmful, and refused to talk. She merely remarked: "I want what I do, and not what I say, to speak for me."

The press continued to be fascinated with Bow. In May, the papers reported cheerily that the actress had at last returned to her normal weight, as they talked of her making a comeback. When her new film for Fox Film Corporation, *Call Her Savage*, was released in December, it was declared a success. But when Bow and her husband arrived to spend Christmas in England she told the *Daily Mirror*: "I am tired of being known as the 'It' girl. That was all very well for a time, but I want people to think of me as an actress, and not merely as a player of one-type parts ... I have spent the last two years on my husband's ranch in Nevada, leading a simply healthy outdoor life – riding, hunting and shooting. I prefer the ranch to Hollywood, and it was only after my manager had spent a year trying to persuade me to make another film that I at last agreed to do this. I am under contract until 1934 to make two more films. After that I don't know what I shall do. I may retire from the screen and go and live on the farm."

Bow made only one more film, *Hoop-La*, in 1933. She retired at the age of 28 and shunned the limelight from then on. Bow gave birth to a son, Tony, in December 1934. A year later, when the *Daily Mirror* published a photo of a plump-faced Bow with her young son it was with the headline "Oh Yes! You Remember Her!" The motherly figure was unrecognizable as Bow the svelte flapper, and she appeared to have aged beyond her years. Sadly, Bow did not get her happy ending. She gave birth to another son in 1938 but eventually began showing symptoms of mental illness, even attempting suicide. The former star became an incurable insomniac, rarely went out and was continually ill. Bow spent some time in psychiatric hospital and was diagnosed as schizophrenic. When she left the institution, she lived as a recluse.

Bow was a talented but vulnerable woman. The pressures of work, fame and riding out the scandal arising from the DeVoe trial proved too much. Her career ended because of the court case, and she never achieved the success of her younger days nor showed a desire to do so. She died forgotten. When the once flamboyant actress passed away suddenly in 1965, aged 60, she was almost alone in the world. Only a hired nurse was there when Bow collapsed from a heart attack in her suburban Culver City home, outside Hollywood. By then, few remembered her as a great star in the film city. Even the police announcing her death said only: "It is a woman identified as Clara Bow."

Like Fatty Arbuckle, Bow experienced the dark side of the publicity machine Hollywood spawned to promote its stars. Trailblazing actors and actresses soon found that their newborn celebrity status could disappear in a frenzy of unwelcome attention if there was a whiff of scandal. They learned how easily something can be overblown to sell newspapers, feeding a growing public appetite for gossip about their favourite film idols.

CHAPTER TWO:

A SHOCK TO THE NATION

When those who hold public office fall from grace, they come under intense scrutiny, from both officialdom and the public. As trusted individuals and often high-flyers, their downfall seems more disgraceful than that of celebrities. The public feels bewildered, stunned and sometimes angry. Confidence is shattered in important institutions, and mistrust and cynicism can take hold. Such individuals do not just suffer personal disgrace, they shame the Establishment. Their actions can have far-reaching and serious consequences.

Perhaps the most famous figure to lose his status as the public's darling is a former monarch who, while unelected, represented an empire and its interests on the eve of the Second World War. The affair of King Edward VIII and the thrice-married American and socialite Wallis Simpson was the great scandal of its time. It split the country, and every parlour and pub became a noisy debating chamber. His abdication in 1936 so that he could marry her astounded the world. It saw him spurned by the royal family and become persona non grata in Britain for decades. From then on known as Edward, Duke of Windsor, he was viewed as a wealthy aristocrat in exile, a Nazi sympathizer and a man who put his love for a woman above that for his country. An uncrowned king, he was destined to spend the rest of his life abroad. His reputation was partially redeemed on his death in 1972, because by then society took a more liberal view of his actions.

Born in 1894, Edward was the youngest son of King George V and Queen Mary. He became Prince of Wales aged 16. As a young man, Edward was in the papers every day. He was photographed playing golf in the baggiest and longest of plus fours, and dancing the night away in evening dress. He was pictured in the far reaches of the British Empire: on a tiger shoot in Nepal, big game hunting in Africa and on his ranch in Canada. The prince was always falling off his horse in the hunting field and there was a fear that he would be killed before he reached the throne. The newspapers' favourite question was: "Should the Prince Hunt?" When the First World War broke out, Edward joined the Armed Forces but, to his regret, the government never let him fight. Nevertheless, he visited the front line as often as he could, and was awarded the Military Cross in 1916.

In the 1920s, Edward was the epitome of the gentleman officer of the First World War. His role in the war had made him popular among veterans of the conflict, and he was pictured as a slim figure in khaki or naval blue saying words of sympathy as he met the war's crippled heroes. He was the leader of the youthful hectic society that had survived the carnage of war –

the era of the "Bright Young People" known for daring pyjama parties with candlelight and champagne. The dapper prince inspired fashion trends for Prince of Wales cloth, the elaborate Windsor tie knot, high-cut collars with evening dress and outrageous Fair Isle pullovers. Yet Edward was more than a charming playboy, he was a symbol of the revolt against the stuffy court of his parents. The prince got on well with radical figures such as Liberal politician David Lloyd-George. Some hoped that, when he ascended to the throne, he would instigate a more adventurous and progressive monarchy.

By the 1930s, the world had changed. This decade saw unemployment in Britain, the Great Depression and the menacing rise of Adolf Hitler in Germany. Fascism reared its ugly head in Britain when Sir Oswald Mosley founded the British Union of Fascists in 1932. Some of the upper classes were attracted to the movement, seeing it as an alternative to Communism. It was in this atmosphere that Edward first met Simpson, in January 1931. Soon, she replaced his previous mistress, Thelma, Viscountess Furness, in his affections. The dandy prince's lifestyle no longer seemed in tune with the times. Behind the scenes, the royal family and the government were worried by what they regarded as his reckless behaviour, including his affairs with married women and inability to settle down. His relationship with the married commoner Simpson, in particular, worried both his family and the government because she appeared to have undue influence over him. Simpson attended a party at Buckingham Palace in 1934, where Edward introduced her to his mother, but his father was outraged and refused to meet her. In 1935, Edward visited Hungary and Simpson appeared with him at various balls in Budapest and elsewhere.

FALLEN IDOLS

When King George V died on 20th January 1936, Edward breached protocol by watching the proclamation of his accession from St James' Palace in the company of the still married Simpson. He appeared to have little interest in his duties, to such an extent that, in the early days of his reign, Conservative politician Neville Chamberlain wrote a memorandum to the prime minister, Stanley Baldwin, urging that the king should "settle down": he should wear drabber clothes, work at his despatch boxes and stop making comments about slums or unemployment. Baldwin suppressed the memorandum. Worse, there were rumours that Hitler's ambassador in London, Joachim von Ribbentrop, moved freely in royal circles and that Simpson had been his lover. There were suspicions that she might pass on confidential information to Germany.

Articles about the couple's relationship were published abroad, particularly in the American press. Censorship kept the British public in the dark: pages were torn from foreign magazines, columns blacked out, and whole issues containing references to the relationship between the king and Simpson were seized. Meanwhile, the British press remained silent about the relationship for the "welfare of the nation and the Empire".

Nevertheless, the truth began to leak out. In May, a Court Circular reported that Simpson had been at a dinner party held by the king at St James' Palace. Two months later, a Court Circular revealed she had been at one of the king's parties. In August, the king went on a five-week Adriatic cruise and the royal party included Simpson. On his return, Simpson spent time with the king at Balmoral in Scotland, and at his home at Fort Belvedere in Windsor Great Park. Tongues wagged and eyebrows were raised. Tourists returning from abroad, particularly from America, carried strange tales. They also brought cuttings from the American press with them, saying "Mrs Simpson is Friend of the King", then "Mrs Simpson is Guest during Edward VIII's Holiday" and, finally, "King to Wed Mrs Simpson". The king was portrayed as Simpson's poodle with headlines like "King Chooses Clothes to Match Mrs Simpson's". She was depicted as ambitious and presumptuous: "Mrs Simpson All Set to Tour Her Empire". Rumours spread, passed from mouth to mouth throughout the country. Slowly, the whispers spread from diplomatic circles, on to banquets, and so to professionals and businessmen.

Simpson gained her decree nisi in October 1936 at Ipswich Assizes. Her petition stated that her marriage was happy until 1934, when her husband, Ernest, began to stay out often at night. Misconduct was alleged between him and a woman at a hotel in Bray-on-Thames earlier that year. Ernest did not defend the petition. The judge was surprised that the case was being heard at Ipswich: the truth was that Simpson had taken up residence in the town temporarily in the hope her divorce would go through swiftly before the British press found out about it. Nevertheless, details of the divorce still made it into the papers. Ernest colluded in the divorce by agreeing to be the wrongdoer rather than allow the king's name to be mentioned in court. A rumour then spread that Ernest had been paid a large sum of money for his silence in the divorce proceedings and for not defending the petition – later this was revealed to be untrue. Simpson worried that the decree absolute would not be allowed, but the king's proctor desisted from interviewing servants that may have led to him having reason to disallow the suit.

Behind the scenes, Baldwin spoke to the king about his relationship with Simpson and his intention to marry her. Yet hopes remained that Edward would prove a positive influence, particularly after he witnessed terrible poverty on a tour to the "black areas" of Wales in November, and said: "Something must be done." The visit was his last public appearance before he abdicated. The same month, the official barriers around the royal romance cracked when questions were put in the House of Commons asking why American magazines imported into the country had been censored. On 1st December, Bradford's Bishop Alfred Blunt appeared to publicly rebuke the king during his diocesan conference. The veil of secrecy was swept aside. Finally, the king's relationship with Simpson and his possible abdication were discussed in the British press.

Edward's failing was that he had no friends in touch with respectable opinion. He thought he could keep his private life distinct from his public one, underestimating the prevailing influence of traditional standards of behaviour. In the late 1930s, the moral stigma of divorce still drove men and women from public life. As king, Edward was the titular head of the Church of England, which took a rigorous stand against divorce. Those who felt he should be able to marry the woman he loved, despite her colourful matrimonial past, argued fiercely with those who thought the dignity of the Crown and the whole future of royalty was doomed. "He should give her up," cried the moralists ranging themselves alongside the entire force of the Establishment, determined to prevent the king from entering into unholy wedlock. "It wouldn't last anyway," said the professional pessimists. They were convinced the romance would be no more than a royal flash-in-the-pan.

There was some effort to drum up support for Edward and even an idea to form a King's Party in parliament, although he found the suggestion abhorrent. Influential press barons Max Aitken, Lord Beaverbrook and Harold Harmsworth, 1st Viscount Rothermere, supported the idea of a morganatic marriage in which Edward would remain king but Simpson would not become queen. However, the British Cabinet and the heads of the Dominion governments in the British colonies took the democratic constitutional view that the king must accept the advice of his ministers. The king's options were to give up Simpson, abdicate or marry against his ministers' wishes. Going against his ministers' advice would cause the government to resign, sparking a constitutional crisis. Edward chose to abdicate.

On 10th December, Edward signed the Instrument of Abdication at 10am in his study on the ground floor of Fort Belvedere. His brother, Prince Albert, Duke of York, succeeded to the throne as King George VI. When Baldwin entered the House of Commons to read Edward's abdication statement he was greeted with cheers. Baldwin delivered it to a hushed chamber, while peeresses and wives of members of parliament sitting in the galleries wept. Later that evening when the House reconvened, the reception was mixed. MPs cheered the leader of the opposition, Clement Atlee, when he said that it was the wish of the people that Edward "may have a long and happy life". Some MPs were less generous, alluding to Simpson's links to Hitler's Germany and the German ambassador, Ribbentrop. One said: "I want to draw attention to the fact that Mrs Simpson has a social set, and every Member of the Cabinet knows that the social set of Mrs Simpson is closely identified with a certain foreign government and the ambassador of that foreign government. [Cries of 'No, no.'] It is common knowledge, and round about this issue is the issue that is continually arising when other [parliamentary] debates come on."

Another MP went a step further, saying: "I have listened to more cant and humbug than I have ever listened to in my life. I have heard praise of the King which was not felt sincerely in any quarter of the House. I go further. Who has not heard the tittle-tattle and gossip that is going about? If he had not voluntarily stepped from the Throne, everyone knows that the same people in the House who pay lip service to him would have poured out scorn, abuse and filth … I have no doubt that you will go on praising the next King as you have praised this one. You will go on telling about his wonderful qualities. If he is a tenth as good as you say, why are you not keeping him? Why is everyone wanting to unload him? Because you know he is a weak creature."

Many in the Establishment did not trust Simpson. They felt she was an unwelcome and possibly dangerous influence on Edward. Nevertheless, many British people took a more positive view of the liaison and were stunned by Edward's abdication because they knew so little of the affair that led to it. A huge throng of people gathered outside the Houses of Parliament to learn if the as yet uncrowned king was to reign or to abdicate in order to marry Simpson – the crowd was so large that mounted police were called in to help control them. At 3pm the crowd had formed an impenetrable mass. Between 3.15pm and 3.30pm, a strange hush fell upon the entire gathering. Suddenly, before the arrival of the evening papers, the news of the abdication spread through the crowd like a flame. Still not a word was said, as people seemed unable to realize that the nation had lost its king.

The sympathies of the men and women in the street on the question of Edward's marriage were with him. In London, newspapers with reports of the latest situation were sold as fast as they could be handed to anxious-faced men and women, office workers, diners and theatregoers. News theatres showing a film of the new "homely" king and queen with their two daughters had a constant stream of patrons. Theatre queues were silent. In Soho, people sat in little groups around café tables discussing one topic. Irish playwright George Bernard Shaw was quick to comment on the announcement – without sentimentality – saying: "The King has abdicated not because of his intention to marry Mrs Simpson, but simply because he hated his job and had enough of it."

The next day, Edward made a radio broadcast to the nation and the British Empire "as a private person owing allegiance to the new King". He explained his decision: "You all know the reasons which have impelled me to renounce the throne. But you must believe me when I tell you that I have found it impossible to carry the heavy burden … and discharge my duties as King without the help and support of the woman I love."

He added: "If at any time I can be found of service to his Majesty … I shall not fail."

King George VI announced his brother would be titled His Royal Highness the Duke of Windsor. By making Edward a royal duke, the king ensured he could not stand for election to parliament, nor speak on political topics in the House of Lords. The country's state of profound confusion at Edward's decision was evident in the words of an article of the time, which talked of the new Duke of Windsor making his "exit of awful silence and embarrassment".

Edward gave up more than a royal crown. He left Britain for Austria and never lived in his native country again. In May 1937, Simpson was divorced. She and the duke married a month later in France. No one from the duke's family attended. Simpson became known as Wallis, Duchess of Windsor, but the royal family refused to confer the title "Her Royal Highness" on the duchess, which remained an "open wound" for the duke throughout his life. In October, the duke and duchess visited Germany, where they met Hitler, without the approval of the British government. The meeting gave credence to the opinion that the couple were Nazi sympathizers. The duke and duchess then settled in France. In 1939, when the Second World War broke out, the duke was appointed governor of the Bahamas. Some have speculated that the posting was intended to keep the couple from harming the war effort.

After the war, the duke and the duchess lived in retirement in France. The duke was never given another official appointment. By the late 1950s, the British press regarded them as a couple of "bores", as they told and retold their story in books and magazine interviews. The couple did the rounds among high society: tea with American gossip columnist Elsa Maxwell, golf with the American pro Arnold Palmer, high jinks off Bermuda, and galas with Princess Grace of Monaco. Yet there was something immensely sad about seeing a man of royal blood mixing with gossip queens and namedroppers. When the couple lived in France, the duke's love for the country of his birth was evident in the possessions he kept around him: the engraved inkstands, cigar boxes and gifts from the past. He made that love clear by requesting that on his death he be buried in English soil.

The duke's wish was granted. In May 1972, he died at his home in Paris at the age of 77. His wife was by his side. His body was returned to Britain for a funeral held at St George's Chapel, Windsor Castle, and he was buried at the Royal Burial Ground, Frogmore Estate, at Windsor. The British government's reaction was respectful – the nation's foremost prodigal son appeared to have been rehabilitated by the Establishment. Prime Minister Edward Heath praised the duke for making the British Empire "a living reality". In his address of sympathy in the House of Commons, Heath said: "By his conduct as Prince of Wales and King, he pointed the way to a form of monarchy which today is more in tune with the times than would have been thought possible fifty-five years ago, when he embarked on his public life. Thus he helped to lay the foundation for the strength of the monarchy today, and for the respect and affection in which the institution and the person of the sovereign are held."

In the last years of the duke's life there was a thaw in relations between him and the royal family. Queen Elizabeth II met the duke in private after she ascended to the throne, but the first time she met the duchess was in 1965, at a London clinic, when the duke was recovering from an operation. In 1969, the queen invited the duke to the Investiture of the Prince of Wales but he declined. After the duke was diagnosed with throat cancer, the queen visited him in May 1972 while on a state visit to France. He died later that month. The 75-year-old duchess stayed at Buckingham Palace during the funeral period at the special invitation of the queen. It was the first time that the duchess had been invited to stay at the palace.

However, even in death it was hard to forget that the duke had fallen from favour. After King Edward VII died in 1910, a tradition had arisen that every British monarch lies in state in Westminster Hall, London, symbolizing the close links between the monarchy and parliament. However, the duke's body lay in state in St George's Chapel, leading some to protest at what appeared to be a royal snub. The British people proved to be more forgiving. Crowds stood in a queue that stretched for more than two miles as they waited to pay a last tribute to the duke – many more than officials expected, causing them to extend the opening hours at the chapel.

After the duke's death, his wife continued to live in Paris. She suffered from ill health in her later years and rarely appeared in public. When she died in 1986, at the age of 89, her body was taken to England, where she was laid to rest alongside her husband. At the duchess' funeral, the press paid close attention to the reaction of her sister-in-law, Queen Elizabeth, the Queen Mother. Many people believed that the Queen Mother had blamed the duchess for the early death of her beloved husband, "Bertie", who was not born to be king and who had physically crumbled under the pressures of being sovereign when he dutifully accepted the crown after his brother's abdication. However, the Queen Mother gave no hint of her feelings for the woman who had changed the course of British history and transformed the personal destiny of each member of the family who were walking behind her coffin.

Thus, history proved the naysayers wrong. The duke and duchess' marriage lasted 35 years. The duke knew that the scandal created by his marriage undermined the solid structure of royalty – a structure that had become so deeply respectable and respected. For a man brought up to value family life, the loss of the close family companionship was a sacrifice. The supreme irony of the life of Edward, Duke of Windsor, is that in contemporary times he might have married the woman of his choice yet still have kept his job and his crown. Whether he would have been the hoped-for radical monarch and continued to hold the love of his subjects through the dark days of the Second World War – given his suspected political leanings – no one knows. In 2013, the government released intelligence files revealing that, at the height of the abdication crisis, ministers had ordered the bugging of his telephones in Buckingham Palace and Fort Belvedere. It is an indication of the level of distrust between the king and his government, and how much his actions threatened the institution of the monarchy.

Sex was to prove a problem for those at the heart of British government itself decades after Edward's abdication when the Profumo affair of 1963 became the biggest political scandal to explode in Britain in a century. It filled the newspapers, absorbed the TV and dominated the nation's conversation. With each new revelation, the story became more incredible and the effects spread, threatening to bring down the government with its revelations of high-society hedonism, lies, adultery, orgies, drugs, guns, call girls, suicide and espionage.

The man at the centre of the scandal was secretary of state for war in Harold Macmillan's Conservative government, John "Jack" Profumo. A rich man, Profumo's barrister dad was an Italian baron, and Profumo himself attended Harrow and Oxford. In 1940, aged 25, he became the House of Commons' youngest MP – he fought in North Africa during the Second World War while still serving as an MP. Profumo was one of the 40 Tory MPs who voted against Neville Chamberlain's government after the Norwegian campaign, helping pave the way for Winston Churchill to become prime minister. Profumo was a privy councillor to Queen Elizabeth II and at one point tipped as a future prime minister.

Profumo's downfall was that he was a charmer who liked the girls. A married man, he had an affair with a call girl and model, Christine Keeler, in 1961. At the same time, Keeler was the mistress of Captain Yevgeni "Eugene" Ivanov, a Russian naval attaché at the Soviet embassy in London and a spy. It was the height of the Cold War and there were fears Profumo had become a blackmail risk.

The war minister first spotted Keeler in July 1961, as she climbed naked out of a swimming pool in the magnificent grounds of the Cliveden estate. The Berkshire mansion belonged to the National Trust, but William Astor, 3rd Viscount Astor, one of the world's richest men and a political power in the land, was the tenant. Lord Astor got to know high-society osteopath and artist Dr Stephen Ward in 1950 when he visited him as a patient. In 1956, Lord Astor let a cottage to Ward on the estate and allowed him to use the pool. Ward used to take pretty girls he met to the cottage at weekends. Ward seduced many of them himself as well as procuring them as mistresses for his influential friends, some of whom had perverted tastes. There is evidence that Ward was ready to arrange for whipping and other sadistic performances. He kept collections of pornographic photos and attended parties where there were orgies.

Ward, the son of a curate at Rochester Cathedral, had brought sultry Keeler with him that day. Keeler had left home at the age of 16 and gone to work as a showgirl at Murray's Cabaret Club, where she met Ward. She lived with Ward for a while at his London home in Wimpole Mews, Marylebone. A society Mr Fixit, Ward took Keeler to the Cliveden cottage frequently, and introduced her to many men, some of rank and position, with whom she had sexual intercourse. He also introduced her to the hemp drug and she became addicted to it. Keeler left the party that day with Ivanov, not Profumo. However, Profumo could not forget the sight of the 19-year-old auburn-haired beauty and asked Ward for her telephone number – this was the beginning of Profumo's sexual relationship with Keeler.

Ward knew Ivanov, who was often at the Cliveden cottage and visited Ward in London. A drinker and ladies' man, Ivanov was keen to meet prominent people in the Establishment. Ward introduced him to many of his high-ranking friends and many girls. However, the British security services discovered that the naval attaché was a Soviet intelligence officer and – the month before Profumo met Keeler – advised Ward of the need for caution.

In August 1961, Profumo broke off his acquaintance with Ward after a warning from MI5 to the cabinet secretary, Sir Norman Brook, saying that the British security services thought Ward might be a security risk because of his friendship with Ivanov. Profumo also broke off his affair with Keeler. Neither the security services nor Brook realized that Profumo knew Keeler.

Profumo's affair may never have come to light but for Keeler's behaviour. She formed a relationship with a Jamaican drug dealer and jazz musician, Aloysius "Lucky" Gordon, which ended acrimoniously. Claiming that Gordon assaulted her and held her hostage, naked, for three days, Keeler sought the protection of another lover, Antiguan jazz promoter Johnny Edgecombe. In October 1962, Gordon was knifed in a fight, leaving him with 17 stitches to his face. Although Edgecombe said he did not know who did it, a warrant was issued for his arrest. Keeler and Edgecombe initially went into hiding in Brentford but then she left, and when Edgecombe sought her help, she refused and said she would give evidence against him. Two months later, on 14th December, an enraged Edgecombe tracked down Keeler at Ward's London mews flat, where she was staying. When she refused to come out of the house, he fired seven shots at the door. Edgecombe was arrested on a charge of attempted murder, although this was later dropped.

When the police probed into the shooting, Keeler told them about Profumo and Ivanov. In January 1963, she went to the press and signed a contract to sell them her story, giving it colour by relating her double life "with rich men in high places and coloured men in low". She told the reporters that Ward had asked her to obtain information as to when the Americans were going to give nuclear weapons to Germany. The same month, Ivanov left London ahead of schedule – it had been expected he would return to Moscow in May.

A newspaper proprietor visited the prime minister's office on 1st February to apprise him of the rumours linking the names of Keeler, Profumo and Ivanov. The press, curbed by tough libel laws, published nothing. When the story was put to Profumo, he admitted he knew Keeler but denied their relationship was anything more than an innocent social friendship.

Afraid of Gordon, Keeler fled to Spain and failed to appear as a witness at Edgecombe's trial at the Old Bailey. The prosecution insisted they had enough to carry on without her. On 15th March, Edgecombe was acquitted of assaulting Gordon but jailed for seven years for possessing a weapon to endanger life. He claims Keeler had bought the gun he used for her protection against Gordon. Edgecombe served five years. The press began to ask why "The Missing Model" Keeler had failed to appear in the witness box. Rumours began to circulate around Fleet Street and Whitehall that Profumo had paid Keeler to vanish.

The first public hint of the scandal came during a debate in the House of Commons on 21st March. Three Labour MPs, George Wigg, Richard Crossman and Barbara Castle, spoke under the protection of parliamentary privilege regarding the rumours connecting a minister to Keeler. Demands for an inquiry ensued. Castle said: "… if it is just a case of a Minister having been found with a pretty girl, good luck to him, but what if there is something else of much greater importance? What if it is a question of the perversion of justice that is at stake … If accusations are made that there are people in high places who do know and who are not informing the police, is it not a matter of public interest?"

The next day, Profumo made a personal statement in the Commons: "It was alleged that people in high places might have been responsible for concealing information concerning the disappearance of a witness, and the perversion of justice. I understand that my name has been connected with the rumours about the disappearance of Miss Keeler."

He went on: "I last saw Miss Keeler in December 1961, and have not seen her since. I have no idea where she is now. Any suggestion that I was in any way connected with, or was responsible for, her absence at the trial at the Old Bailey is wholly and completely untrue."

Profumo explained: "My wife and I had a standing invitation to visit Dr Ward, and between July and December, 1961, I met Miss Keeler on about a dozen occasions at Dr Ward's flat when I called to see him and his friends."

Speaking with deliberation, Profumo told the MPs: "Miss Keeler and I were on friendly terms. There was no impropriety in my acquaintanceship with Miss Keeler."

Profumo ended with the challenge: "I shall not hesitate to issue writs for libel and slander if scandalous allegations are made or repeated outside this House."

The fact that Macmillan sat beside Profumo during his statement was seen as an indication of the premier's full personal confidence in the war minister. The government's view was that Profumo's denial of the allegations closed the matter. There was no question of him resigning from government, and there were even cheers when he finished his statement.

At the same time, Ward told the police of Keeler's whereabouts. On 24th March, the British Embassy in Madrid contacted her. She returned to England the following month. On 7th May, Ward requested an interview with the prime minister's principal private secretary, T J Bligh, during which he alleged that what Profumo said in the Commons was, in certain respects, untrue. Ward also sent a letter in a similar vein to the home secretary, Henry Brooke. Ward's allegations were put to Profumo but he insisted his statement was true.

On 4th June, while the prime minister was on holiday, Profumo asked for a meeting with Bligh and the government chief whip, Martin Redmayne. He told them he had not told the truth and wanted to resign. Profumo did so the same day via a dramatic letter to the prime minister, admitting that he had lied to the Commons about his association with Keeler and reassuring him that no breach of security took place: "In my statement I said that there had been no impropriety in this association. To my deep regret, I have to admit that this was not true and that I misled you and my colleagues and the House. I ask you to understand that I did this to protect, as I thought, my wife and family, who were equally misled, as were my professional advisers. I have come to realise that, by this deception, I have been guilty of a grave misdemeanour, and despite the fact that there is no truth whatsoever in the other charges, I cannot remain a member of your administration, nor of the House of Commons. I cannot tell you of my deep remorse for the embarrassment I have caused you, to my colleagues in the Government, to my constituents and to the Party I have served for the past twenty-five years."

Profumo's glittering career was over at 48. His actress wife, Valerie Hobson, star of Ealing comedies such as *Kind Hearts and Coronets*, stood by him loyally. Profumo's resignation reflected badly on Macmillan, who had swallowed the lie, and Macmillan's ability to govern was called into question because it was obvious he did not have the slightest idea how one of his prominent ministers was conducting himself. The Labour opposition in government wanted an investigation of reports that security men knew both Profumo and Ivanov were visiting Keeler. The public were aghast when a friend of Keeler's, 19-year-old Marilyn "Mandy" Rice-Davies, revealed: "The farcical thing about it all was that on more than one occasion – as Jack left Christine at the flat where she stayed, Eugene walked in. In fact it was something of a standing joke among us."

The country appeared to be in crisis as the details of the scandal – and its implications – unravelled rapidly. On 8th June, Ward was arrested and accused of living on the immoral earnings of prostitution. He was sent to Brixton Prison and refused bail, pending more serious charges. Two days later, the London Stock Exchange slumped as the scandal sliced millions of pounds off share values. Lord Dilhorne, the lord chancellor, prepared a secret report into the security side of the affair. Labour leader Harold Wilson had sent other reports about Ivanov's activities to the prime minister several weeks earlier. There were signs of growing pressure among Conservative MPs for a new leader who could restore their party's moral image in the eyes of the nation.

Dilhorne's report was delivered to the Cabinet but not published. Wilson also received a copy. The government's morality was on trial and one church leader spoke out, criticizing "the smell of corruption in high places, of evil practices, and of a repudiation of the simple decencies and the basic values". Later, Macmillan told astonished MPs that the security services had not passed reports on to him that Keeler had been asked to obtain certain information from Profumo when he was war minister. He revealed that British security agents took a statement from Keeler in January. Keeler stated that on one occasion when she was going to meet Profumo, Ward had asked her to discover some information but that she had not put the question to Profumo. The security risk was revealed to have been minor and

Macmillan survived as leader of the government.

On 21st June, Macmillan asked a judge, Alfred, Lord Denning, to lead an inquiry into the circumstances leading to Profumo's resignation. The same month, Gordon was jailed for three years for assaulting Keeler, but she subsequently withdrew her accusations and was convicted for perjury six months later. Profumo lost his final honour in late June when, at his request, his name was struck from the Roll of Privy Councillors.

In July, the scandal reached a climax with the Old Bailey trial of Ward. He was arraigned on five counts: three for living off immoral earnings, the fourth for procurement, and the fifth for attempting to procure. The country, still emerging from the austere postwar years of the 1940s and 1950s, was stunned to hear of the goings-on at Cliveden. One prosecution witness, 20-year-old prostitute Vickie Barrett, told the court she sometimes caned men and horsewhipped them at Ward's flat. When the prosecution pointed out to Rice-Davies that Lord Astor denied an affair or having even met her, she said: "He would, wouldn't he?"

When 50-year-old Ward was out on bail during the trial, he took a massive overdose of sleeping pills and was found unconscious at a friend's flat. Ward lingered in a coma for three days as the jury found him guilty on two counts of living off the immoral earnings of Keeler and Rice-Davies. On 3rd August he died in hospital, having never regained consciousness. One of Ward's last actions before he took his life was to phone the Home Office official who was helping Denning in his inquiry. Later that month, a judge ruled that Ward's literary agent could not publish Ward's memoirs.

Since then, some have claimed that Ward surrounded himself with girls for pleasure, not profit, and that his was a tale of immorality, rather than crime. In June 1963, when Ward was first questioned by the police during the vice probe, he said officials followed "a certain line of questioning which disturbed me deeply ... The line seemed to indicate that somehow I had been living on immoral earnings, or introduced people to men, for money."

It has been argued that the case against Ward was feeble, consisted of uncorroborated statements by proven liars, and that the reason so many charges were brought was in the hope that one or two of them would stick. Some suggest that the press coverage of the Profumo affair, combined with unconscious political pressure to restore the government's good name, meant Ward became the whipping boy for the humiliations the government suffered because of the scandal. It has even been suggested that Ward worked for MI5 and had been tasked with turning Ivanov into a double agent. Whatever the truth, Ward's death meant he became a convenient scapegoat for the Establishment.

Proof of the grip the scandal had on the public came in September, when Lord Denning published his 50,000-word report, detailing his findings. People queued at midnight to make sure of a copy, and some 100,000 copies were sold at seven shillings and sixpence each. In compiling the report, the judge heard 160 witnesses, including Prime Minister Macmillan and eight cabinet ministers.

Denning exonerated the security services, saying they he did "not think they should be blamed for not doing more" and there was "no reason to believe that there was any security leakage whatever". He described Profumo's conduct as disclosing a "character defect" that pointed to his being a security risk. He concluded that Ivanov may have used Ward as a "tool" to make friends with prominent people. The report criticized Macmillan and his colleagues for not dealing more effectively with the situation that arose through Profumo's association with Keeler. However, Denning found some words of compassion for Keeler: "Let no one judge her too harshly ... Since the age of sixteen she had become enmeshed in a net of wickedness ..."

The report was a best-seller despite being hailed as a whitewash. Denning refuted the accusation, saying morality was outside the scope of the report: "It is, I believe, better for the country that these rumours should be buried and this unfortunate episode should be closed."

Macmillan resigned a month later because of ill health, although the scandal may have attributed to his demise. His party lost the 1964 general election to Labour. Although there was no evidence Profumo let slip military secrets during pillow talk, and did not know he was sharing his mistress' bed with Ivanov, the scandal was so salacious no politician had a hope of surviving once the details emerged. Without the scandal, Profumo would have served his country well. It is often said it was not sleeping with Keeler that cost him his career – it was lying about it to the House of Commons. As an MP, Profumo turned into a disaster zone for his party. He made a very human error and afterwards attempted to make up for it with an act of atonement, devoting his life to charity by working in the East End of London for the homeless, the poor and the dispossessed. He washed dishes, raised funds and tried to help addicts to recover. For his efforts, Profumo was appointed a commander of the British Empire in 1975. The honour signalled both his return to respectability and the fact that the Establishment had forgiven his sins. However, his exploits were later portrayed in the 1988 film about the affair, *Scandal*, helping ensure his name would be forever associated with sleaze.

When Profumo died in 2006 at the age of 91, Prime Minister Tony Blair said: "He made a serious mistake, but then underwent a journey of redemption in which he gave support and help to many, many people." A spokesman for Toynbee Hall, the East End charity where Profumo worked for so many years, told the *Daily Mirror*: "He was our longest-serving volunteer. John Profumo was a wonderful man who was very kind and got on well with people of all levels. He was very much admired and loved."

Just 10 years after the Profumo affair, the British government was mired in another grubby story of sleazy sex. Conservative air force minister, Lord Lambton, caused a scandal when he was photographed smoking cannabis in bed with two call girls in 1973. The revelation led to his resignation from Edward Heath's government. Photographs of the wealthy aristocrat in his trademark dark glasses were splashed across the pages of newspapers that summer. He had been careless, arriving for appointments with a popular dominatrix to the rich in a chauffeur-driven Daimler, and even paying for her services by cheque.

Born in 1922, Antony Lambton married Belinda Blew-Jones in 1942, and the couple went on to have six children. Antony became an MP in 1951. After his father's death in 1970 he was briefly 6th Earl of Durham, but he disclaimed his title to pursue his political career as MP for Berwick-upon-Tweed, although he insisted on being called by his courtesy title, Viscount

Lambton, and being referred to as "Lord" not "Mr".

The chain of events that led to Lambton's disgrace began in February 1972 when Scotland Yard began checking on a porn king, James Humphrey, who owned strip clubs and pornographic bookshops in London's Soho. They were looking into allegations of a close friendship between him and a senior police officer. During the six-week inquiry, police discovered that Humphrey kept a diary in which he recorded the names of all the people he met. The diary led to police mounting massive raids in January 1973. Detectives swooped on Soho bookshops, clip joints and Mayfair clubs, seizing books, magazines, photographs – and lists of names. In April, the leads in the diary pointed to a model agency, and the trail led from there to Lambton.

Meanwhile, photographs of Lambton and a model at the agency, 26-year-old Norma Levy, were touted around Fleet Street. In fact, Norma was a call girl. Her husband Colin had used a camera hidden behind a peephole in a mirror to photograph Lambton in bed with his wife and another woman, Kim Pinder, at their flat in Maida Vale, London. Lambton was also photographed smoking marijuana. Colin Levy walked into the offices of the *News of the World* with the photographs in an envelope. The newspaper's reporters and editor studied the photographs, but did not hand over any money or make any promises to the man. The *News of the World* then called Scotland Yard. Metropolitan Police Commissioner Sir Robert Mark put two of his top detectives on the case.

In late May, a leak to the German magazine *Stern* started the final turn of the screw when it published a report linking a British aristocrat with a sex scandal. The magazine said it knew the name of the man but refused to identify him. After *Stern* published the story, police visited the 50-year-old Lambton. They told him Colin Levy had taken secret photographs and tried to sell them to newspapers. The next day, Lambton quit his job.

Lambton issued a statement revealing the sordid story behind his resignation. He admitted that in the previous few months he had had a "casual acquaintance with a call girl and one or two of her friends". Lambton spoke of the crisis he faced when police told him the call girl's husband had taken secret photographs and tried to sell them to newspapers. He said: "This is the sordid story. There has been no security risk and no blackmail and never at any time have I spoken of any aspect of my late job. All that has happened is that some sneak pimp has seen the opportunity of making money by the sale of the story and secret photographs to papers at home and abroad."

Within hours of his statement, news came from the Attorney General's office that Lambton was being accused of offences under the Dangerous Drugs Act. Senior Scotland Yard officers were granted summonses concerning the possession of cannabis and amphetamines. Lambton talked about drugs in a second statement issued through his agent: this declared suspicions that Lambton was a drug addict were unfounded. The statement talked about the police visit to Lambton: "They appeared to believe I was a heroin addict and asked to inspect the veins on my arms and legs. I consented. They were unmarked. They then asked to search my house. I willingly complied and showed them at once a small parcel of soft drugs that I had confiscated from a friend many months ago. They also found barbiturate pills which I have had, on and off, on prescription for fifteen years."

Lambton added: "If I had had any sense of guilt I had ample time to hide the pills. I made no attempt to do so."

The same day, it was revealed that two top civil servants had been named in a secret police dossier on vice-ring allegations being probed by Scotland Yard. The name of a leading Tory politician was linked with the inquiry. The civil servants worked in a government department closely associated with military secrets, although there was no suggestion that either had parted with confidential information. The police report was handed to the home secretary. The report suggested that the two men were present at parties at which photographs were taken without their knowledge. The pictures were said to show them in embarrassing situations.

Within days of Lambton's resignation, the leader of the Lords and Lord Privy Seal, George Jellicoe, 2nd Earl Jellicoe, quit after admitting to using prostitutes, although he did not know Norma. The scandal came close to bringing down Heath's government. When a by-election was held to fill Lambton's old seat, the Tories lost to a Liberal candidate. At the time, there were rumours of another government minister being involved with call girls – some official papers pertaining to the scandal have still not been released.

A "torture chamber" for sadomasochistic sex was found in Norma's Maida Vale flat. She kept whips, masks, manacles, rubber and leather clothing, a stock of blue films and a projector. Illicit sex and the blackmail that might follow it are key weapons in wars of espionage. The Cold War was being played out at the time of the scandal, and German spy trials had indicated that sex tactics in the security world usually centred around high-grade call girls or independent female operators planted by a foreign power. The government was concerned that state secrets may have been leaked to the prostitutes. The press revealed that special MI5 agents known as the "Faceless Ones" had been working for three months to gain information on international vice rings and the prominent British politicians and businessmen who used them. The Faceless Ones were active in London's Mayfair. They reported on a number of men who were having parties with women and then disappearing to various flats.

In June, the *News of the World* admitted it took secret photographs of Lambton with two call girls. The newspaper said that the pictures were not intended for publication but were taken to check their informant's allegations. A debate ensued on whether the government should toughen anti-snooping laws. Lambton said he was "very surprised" at their actions, adding: "It is a funny business." Despite the press intrusion, Lambton denied that the *News of the World* had invaded his privacy. In an interview for American TV, he said he did not agree with some newspaper comment that he suffered a worse fate than he deserved. He said: "There is nothing in this country to stop a newspaper being asked into a house and taking photographs of anyone there ... There would be a great danger if the press was curbed and felt it couldn't inquire into certain things."

In June, a commission was set up to probe into aspects of the scandal in order to verify that Lambton and Lord Jellicoe's associations with the call girls had not endangered national security. The same month, Lambton pleaded guilty to three charges of possessing drugs and incurred a fine of £300. The court heard that police asked Lambton whether Norma had given him drugs. He said she had given him pep pills "but I had never taken them". Lambton said that in the past he had smoked marijuana and had smoked opium in China. When Lambton was asked if he had requested drugs on any visit to Norma's flat he said he had talked about them, saying: "It was a fetish with me. It was my fetish to talk about drugs when I got to bed. It was all a game we played."

Lambton was shown a photograph of himself on the bed at Norma's flat, smoking. The police said it showed him smoking cannabis. He replied: "I would not deny that. I would not deny that I have smoked marijuana."

The court heard that when police officers went to Lambton's home in St John's Wood, London, they found cannabis and amphetamine tablets in a drawer built into the skirting board in his bedroom. More cannabis was found in the bathroom cupboard. There were more tablets in a bottle on a table. When Lambton showed the police the cannabis and tablets in the skirting board he said: "You had better have this."

He was asked: "Are you saying this is yours, or are you looking after it for somebody else?"

Lambton said: "I accept responsibility for it."

The defence stated that Lambton had taken the drugs into his care "to prevent their use by another person"; that he did not wish to disclose their identity, and that he claimed the drugs were neither for his use nor consumption. The prosecution was unable to accept this. Its inquiries found that Lambton asked associates for drugs and they gave them to him: "The same witnesses said on one or more occasions he was in possession of cannabis and had, in fact, smoked it."

After the scandal, Lambton became a writer and columnist. He went to live at his 17th-century villa in Tuscany, Italy, earning him the nickname the "King of Chiantishire". His marriage was ruined but he never divorced, although he lived at the villa with his companion, Claire Ward. A rich man, Lambton survived the scandal but lost a promising career. He appeared to endure the consequences of his actions with dignity, yet there is little doubt he suffered. When Sir Robin Day interviewed Lambton, after he resigned, for the TV show *Panorama*, the former politician told his host casually that he had used "whores for sex" because "I think people sometimes like variety". Later, Day said that Lambton was the most difficult person he had ever interviewed: "This was clearly a matter of public interest but one had to approach it from the point of view of a man whose career had been shattered and who had very personal and very painful problems."

In 2004, secret government papers released to the National Archives revealed that during a security probe Lambton told MI5 officer Charles Elwell he had turned to vice girls because he was bored by the "futility" of his job as a government minister. Lambton had thrown himself into a "frenzied round of vigorous gardening and debauchery" after losing a three-year battle over the use of his father's title. However, the MI5 officer said he believed the scandal had driven Lambton "to the verge of collapse". Lambton described the London flat where he was photographed as "the scene of great debauchery".

When the scandal broke, call girl Norma and her husband Colin fled to Europe. After a drunken row, Colin allegedly attempted to run over his wife in a Mercedes. He was arrested in Spain but charges were dropped. When Colin was arrested, police had seized his briefcase, which was said to hold the key to other names behind the Lambton affair. It was reported to contain tape recordings, pornographic photographs and other pictures. Norma returned to Britain where she stood trial. She revealed that she ran a vice ring and got off with a £225 fine for influencing the movements of prostitutes. She and Colin divorced. However, Norma continued to make headlines. The widow of Indonesia's President Sukarno started a libel action over her book *I, Norma Levy*. A friend jumped to her death from an eighth-floor window while writing another book about Norma. It was even alleged that Norma masterminded group sex orgies in a private Boeing 707 commuting between Europe and America. Norma went to live in America but was exposed as a prostitute and an illegal immigrant hiding behind a smokescreen of 19 aliases, who ran a 26-strong call-girl ring in Florida. In 1998, the Federal Bureau of Investigation (FBI) caught up with her. She was sent to prison for 18 months and then deported.

There have been suggestions that Lambton was the victim of a set-up and that British secret services supplied Colin with the sophisticated equipment to photograph him. In 2004, the *Mail on Sunday* printed an article claiming that former MI6 operative Lee Tracey had confessed to playing a role in the sting. The newspaper said that Tracey's superiors were determined to unmask Lambton and embarrass MI5, which had failed to act against his activities despite knowing about them. Supposedly, MI6 was concerned with wayward politicians and the possibility they were open to blackmail. Tracey said that he had supplied a night-vision lens to the *News of the World*, which allowed the newspaper's photographer to snap Lambton with Norma. In 2007, Norma told the *Daily Mail* that she doubted

Colin had the expertise to set up the hidden camera positioned behind a stereo system in a wardrobe facing her bed. A listening device was also embedded in the nose of Norma's teddy bear to record Lambton's voice. The newspaper said it knew the name of the third minister said to be involved but would not divulge it, choosing to describe him as "today one of Britain's most respected and best-known elder statesmen and was then a junior minister in the Heath government".

Lambton denied revealing any state secrets. Whether he was the sacrificial victim of a honey trap is unknown. He was rehabilitated by the Establishment: among high-profile guests to his Villa Cetinale home were Prime Minister Tony Blair and his wife Cherie, who had dinner there in 2004. Lambton died in 2006, aged 84. Obituaries talked of the scandal that had held a nation transfixed in the summer of 1973, and a man whose career was cut short by his own weakness.

Only a year after the Lambton scandal, the British government came under pressure when MP John Stonehouse did a Reggie Perrin vanishing act. Stonehouse was a flawed character whose life was the stuff of tragedy. A sophisticated and skilful confidence trickster, Stonehouse was a Labour minister when he faked his own drowning off a Miami beach in 1974 to escape massive debts. Later, he was arrested in Australia, taken to Britain and jailed for seven years for forgery, theft and fraud.

A man with undoubted talent and drive, Stonehouse had the full armoury of the conman: charm, good looks and apparent sincerity. He was an accomplished actor, who slipped easily into his different roles. People believed in him. Stonehouse scaled the heights of government as minister of posts and telecommunications. He became a privy councillor, president of the London Co-operative Society, and persuaded businessmen to invest in his fringe bank.

Stonehouse became a Labour MP in 1957 at 32, first for Wednesbury in Staffordshire and later for Walsall North. In 1964, he tasted real power for the first time when Prime Minister Harold Wilson appointed him as parliamentary secretary at the Aviation Ministry, he went on to become a minister. A succession of posts followed. However, in 1969, his political fortunes faded. As postmaster-general, Stonehouse mishandled a postal dispute early that year – worse, he misled the Cabinet. Wilson was furious. From then on, Wilson considered Stonehouse unreliable and told Cabinet colleagues there would be no place for him in any future Labour administration. After Labour lost the general election in June 1970, Stonehouse set out to make his fortune. Despite the setbacks to his career, he was still an MP and even believed he would one day be prime minister. At the time, Stonehouse explained that he wanted a financial base to make him "totally independent".

Stonehouse was aware of business practice. He had a degree from the London School of Economics and he had also run a co-operative of farmers in Uganda. He set up four companies, Export Promotion and Consultancy Services, London Capital Group (initially called the British Bangladesh Trust), Global Imex and Connoisseurs of Claret. Stonehouse then developed a complex set-up of different companies and bank accounts in order to arrange fraudulent credit, give £729,000-worth of personal guarantees, and run up £375,000-worth of debts with 17 banks on 24 separate accounts, while leaving his main company, Export Promotion and Consultancy Services, penniless.

In 1972, Stonehouse saw his chance to cash in on a boom in fringe banks and so formed the British Bangladesh Trust. The bank needed £500,000 from investors, but it did not attract enough support. Stonehouse started switching cash from company to company to help make up the shortfall. Investors' money intended for the British Bangladesh Trust was lent to other Stonehouse companies, which then put the money in the Trust. Stonehouse also borrowed heavily from banks. It all had the appearance of respectability. Even the books of the Stonehouse bank were dressed up to disguise the shaky foundation of the business.

Stonehouse recorded a loan for a young dressmaker, Susan Hill, whom he had met via his eldest daughter, Jane. The loan looked good on paper and Hill "borrowed" more than £20,000. In fact, no money changed hands. Stonehouse told Hill her name was only being used in shares deal and it meant no financial involvement. She trusted him and he conned her. In the middle of 1974, the auditors – watchdogs on company activities – started to dig deeper into the MP's affairs. They investigated a number of "loans" and found that Hill was not the only one who had been hoodwinked. Stonehouse had used the same trick on an old RAF pal, and even a member of his own family.

Faced with the disastrous consequences of a stern rap by the auditors, Stonehouse took fright and hatched a plan to disappear with his mistress and secretary, Sheila Buckley. Stonehouse was married with three children: 24-year-old Jane, 21-year-old Julia and 14-year-old Matthew. It was then that he pulled his meanest trick: taking over the identities of two men, Joseph Markham and Donald Mildoon, who had died; he spent months rehearsing his new identities. Stonehouse siphoned off nearly £30,000 from Export Promotion and Consultancy Services and set up an elaborate network of bank accounts in Britain and aboard. He accumulated a nest egg for his new life that police at the time estimated was worth £125,000. By late 1974, the MP was under enormous pressure. Banks were calling him to task. Cheques were bouncing and he was being told he could not cash any more. He took out £119,000-worth of insurance policies on his own life, closed down a Westminster flat used by Buckley, and put his £80,000 house in Wiltshire – which was in his wife's name although his family never lived there – up for sale. The time had come to go: Stonehouse left for America.

On 20th November, Stonehouse faked his own death by drowning, at a beach at the plush Fontainebleau Hotel in Miami, Florida. Immediately, his death looked suspicious. On the day he disappeared, his behaviour was strange and he had made a point of leaving his clothing with the beach-club secretary at the hotel, saying: "Remember me ... Could you do me ... [a] favour and look after my clothes while I go for a swim?"

Two lifeguards were baffled because they had not seen him on the quarter-mile stretch of beach that day and did not believe he had drowned. The mystery deepened when coastguards said that any body would normally have surfaced within days, and when a massive air and sea search failed to find any trace of Stonehouse. His shocked wife, Barbara, revealed he was a strong swimmer. The MP's mother, Rosina, was convinced she had lost her son, saying: "I have no doubt that John is dead. It is a great tragedy."

The sea search was widened. As the days went by, doubts grew in the mind of police, led by veteran detective Lieutenant Jack Webb: "I don't like this case. There are easy answers to some things, such as the definite time he was last seen. But then nothing ... The likelihood is that Mr Stonehouse drowned. But I want to keep an open mind. There is just a possibility he is alive, maybe even suffering from loss of memory."

Stonehouse had made the trip to America without telling government whips and was due to be "disciplined" on his return. The press began to scrutinize Stonehouse's business dealings, revealing that four top directors in his companies had resigned recently. As speculation mounted that he was involved in "nefarious activities", one of his friends suggested that he may have been "destroyed by the mafia" because "he was a man not prepared to involve himself in anything dishonourable". Meanwhile, Scotland Yard started to investigate Stonehouse's business dealings and people began to reveal he owed them money. The search intensified and FBI agents dug up a car park looking for his remains. They discovered a concrete coffin, but the corpse inside was not that of Stonehouse.

Matters took an even more bizarre turn when, a month after Stonehouse's disappearance, Josef Frolík, a high-ranking Czech intelligence agent who had defected to the West, claimed Stonehouse had been a contact for a Communist spy ring in the 1960s. Some then wondered if the MP was still alive and had been taken to the USSR. The prime minister dismissed the allegations in a statement to the Commons. Years later, Frolík's accusation was revealed to have weight – that MI5 had suspected

Stonehouse but had insufficient evidence to bring the MP to trial at the time.

In fact, Stonehouse had checked into the luxurious Sheraton Waikiki Hotel in Honolulu, Hawaii, under the name of Joseph Markham. He spent a few days there, taking a sauna, eating in a Polynesian restaurant and living it up in a nightclub. Stonehouse then skipped to Australia, entering the country on a passport under Joseph Markham's name. His faked demise was part of an elaborate plan to start a new life on the other side of the world with his accomplice and lover Buckley, who he kept in touch with by phone at a hotel in Hampstead, London, where she was living. They also met secretly in Copenhagen, Denmark, for a weekend.

On Christmas Eve, after an Australian detective read about Stonehouse in the *Daily Mirror*, police arrested him in Melbourne as a suspected illegal immigrant. By then, Stonehouse was using the false name of Donald Mildoon. He told police he vanished because of pressures and was being blackmailed. He requested permission to stay in Australia permanently. His wife flew out for a Boxing Day reunion behind the high wire of a detention centre with security men close by – she appeared to have no idea about her husband's mistress.

Markham and Mildoon's wives were horrified, and revealed how Stonehouse had got the details he needed for his impersonations. He visited Mildoon's widow in June, a month after her husband had died. She and her late husband were Stonehouse's constituents. The MP extracted information from the bereaved woman about her husband by saying that he was preparing a parliamentary bill about one-parent families. He also visited Markham's widow to do the same, pretending he was doing a survey on pensions.

The police in Australia released Stonehouse. Six weeks later, the love triangle was complete, when Buckley flew to Australia and the waiting arms of her "dearest Dums". Inevitably, the threesome was an unhappy one. Barbara tolerated the presence of her husband's mistress after he threatened to commit suicide if she left him. Meanwhile, Scotland Yard's fraud squad had uncovered massive evidence of theft and fraud within the Stonehouse business complex. After weeks of courtroom wrangling, Stonehouse and Buckley were extradited. They flew back to Britain on 15th July 1975.

After release from Brixton Prison on bail, the runaway MP made a personal statement in the House of Commons. MPs ignored him as he left the chamber. Later, the deputy speaker ordered him out during a debate. Stonehouse became what one commentator described as "a strange and disturbing figure on Britain's political scene". The MP claimed to have undergone a period of philosophical reassessment during his time in Australia: "I have always been an idealist, you know. Always. And in Australia I looked more inwardly. I have even written a book about these thoughts. And it is called *The Last Idealist*."

Stonehouse became increasingly critical of the Labour Party. Three weeks before his trial at the Old Bailey, he quit to join the English National Party, causing further embarrassment to the government. In doing so, Stonehouse placed his old party in a predicament because Prime Minister Jim Callaghan was left leading a minority government. Stonehouse said he felt it was his duty to force a general election. A week before his trial, he sacked his barrister and decided to defend himself. He announced: "As this is a political trial, brought for political reasons, I have decided to defend myself. I want the jury and the country to know the truth, and I feel I am the only person who can put that across."

When the 50-year-old truant MP went to trial on 27th April 1976, he was the first privy councillor in modern times to face a criminal trial. Stonehouse faced 21 charges including conspiracy, fraud, forgery and theft. The prosecution told of how Stonehouse got the addresses of recently bereaved widows from a hospital in his constituency by saying he wanted to help them financially. He visited the widows of Markham and Muldoon and learned enough about the dead men to obtain duplicates of their birth certificates. Stonehouse then opened bank accounts in their names, and obtained a passport in Markham's name. His 29-year-old lover, Buckley, faced six charges of theft and conspiracy.

The former government minister told the jury that he feared disgrace and had fled Britain because he was afraid of "the death of a thousand stabs". His pleas were ignored. On 6th August, 21 months after his disappearance, the axe finally fell. Stonehouse was sentenced to seven years in prison on 18 charges of forgery, theft and fraud. Buckley was convicted of five theft charges. She was given a two-year suspended sentence for her part in her lover's get-rich-quick schemes. The Old Bailey judge told her: "You were unfortunate to meet this persuasive, deceitful and ambitious man."

Stonehouse always insisted that his actions were those of a man driven to a mental breakdown by the destruction of his political ideals. He drew a sympathetic portrait of himself as a fugitive from humbug and hypocrisy, as if he were a disillusioned idealist, torn by the death of his dream. In fact, he was guilty of the very offences he condemned. Shortly before his trial he told the *Daily Mirror*: "What have I done – have I mugged anyone, have I killed anyone? I have done nobody any harm, yet they all want me to get the seven years."

Stonehouse served three years and eight days of his seven-year sentence before he was released on parole. While in jail, his wife divorced him. The saga took its toll on Stonehouse: he had three heart attacks and major surgery while in prison. However, he was not entirely shunned. Although the judge at the trial had told Buckley to "Go away and forget this man", she could not. Buckley stood by Stonehouse – they married in 1981 and went on to have a son.

On his release, Stonehouse took up writing. His first novel, *Ralph*, was a thriller. It told the story of a Eurocrat broken by pressure from a blackmailing East German agent who plans to leave his successful career and family to escape with his beautiful mistress to another identity and country. Comparisons with Stonehouse were unavoidable but he insisted the novel was not based on his own experiences. By 1982, he was attempting to promote a new, improved version of himself, saying: "That other Stonehouse was a different man. That man has gone. I look back on him and shudder. My ambition, my ideas, my appetite for power, they've gone too. Burned out. Now I have tranquillity and peace. Rather like having two different lives."

Stonehouse died from a heart attack in 1988 at the age of 62. His second wife attended the funeral. His first wife Barbara was too ill to attend, but her children by Stonehouse were all there. Barbara said she hoped his political achievements – he introduced first- and second-class postage and, as aviation minister, signed a deal with Airbus – would be remembered rather than his fall from grace. Stonehouse had long hoped that time would bring forgiveness; his family certainly continued to love him despite his disgrace. Reflecting on his past at one point, he said: "I didn't commit any serious crime or hurt anyone."

Of course, political skulduggery occurs the world over. America was left reeling when President Richard Nixon became the only president to ever resign. He did so in 1974 in the face of impeachment, after revelations regarding the Watergate scandal and the misconduct of members of his administration. Known as "Tricky Dicky", during investigations into the affair he famously went on TV to declare: "There can be no whitewash at the White House." He went from being the most powerful man in the world to being outed as a lying crook, who shamed himself, his party and his country.

Nixon was toppled thanks to the efforts of two journalists from the *Washington Post*, Carl Bernstein and Bob Woodward, who broke the story. The duo exposed a network of political spying and intrigue that outraged America. Their dogged reporting revealed how, in the run-up to the 1972 election, Nixon authorized a break-in at the headquarters of the Democratic National Committee in the Watergate office complex in Washington DC. The reporters had help from a secret source, mysteriously referred to as "Deep Throat", whom they met in underground car parks, and with whom they shared whispered phone conversations. He advised them to "follow the money" – a trail that finally led all the way to the White House.

FALLEN IDOLS

Speculation about the identity of "Deep Throat" ranged across characters such as General Alexander Haig and even Secretary of State Henry Kissinger. Woodward and Bernstein – the only ones who knew, along with *Washington Post* editor Ben Bradlee – said they would not reveal the identity of "Deep Throat" until the whistleblower was dead. However, in 2005, the former number two at the Federal Bureau of Investigation, Associate Director W Mark Felt, revealed he was the gravel-voiced informant in an interview with magazine *Vanity Fair*. Felt was a J Edgar Hoover mob-buster. As deputy to Hoover's successor, he became very disturbed by the tactics of Nixon's hirelings, including those of the Watergate burglars. The FBI came under pressure to drop inquiries and Felt realized he was again confronting the mentality of organized crime, this time in the White House. So he began the leaks that would do the job the FBI was not.

Thanks to Felt, a criminal conspiracy was detected and its leaders removed. By the time Bernstein and Woodward's exposés were over, 40 government officials had been indicted – President Nixon resigned in August 1974. Bernstein and Woodward's reports won them a Pulitzer, the highest prize in American journalism. The newsmen's book of the story was even turned into an Oscar-winning film, *All the President's Men*.

The scandal began when five men were arrested for breaking and entering at the DNC headquarters at Watergate on 17th June 1972. They intended to photograph documents and install bugging devices. The FBI found a connection between cash found on the burglars to a slush fund used by the Committee for the Re-Election of the President (CRP), which was a fundraising group for the Nixon campaign. All of the burglars had links to the CRP. The FBI found that the break-in was part of a campaign of espionage and sabotage conducted for the Nixon re-election committee. Nixon was re-elected as president on 7th November.

By the spring of 1973, it emerged that White House officials were involved in a cover-up and the Senate Watergate Committee was set up to investigate the incident. In July 1973, the committee revealed that Nixon had had listening devices installed in the White House and his private office to record various conversations. The recordings showed that Nixon had attempted to cover up illegal activity that had occurred during his administration, both before and after the break-in. Initially, Nixon would not hand over the tapes, citing his executive privilege as president. A court battle ensued to make Nixon hand over the tapes that would implicate him, and the US Supreme Court ruled that the president had to hand them over to government investigators.

When the edited transcripts of the tapes were released in April 1974, they revealed Nixon as a devious, foul-mouthed, vindictive individual. Many in his own Republican Party called for him to step down. The public and the media called for his resignation or impeachment. In late July, the White House released the subpoenaed tapes. On 5th August, the so-called "Smoking Gun" tape was made public, which revealed that Nixon had been involved in an attempted cover-up from the start. He had protested his innocence for nearly two years but all the time he had lied to the country, his aides and his lawyers. During that time, the nation had been tormented by the problem of getting rid of him. Nixon had sanctioned paying hush money to the Watergate burglars to ensure their silence and was involved in a criminal conspiracy in an attempt to obstruct justice. Unsurprisingly, Nixon's support evaporated and he faced certain impeachment. On 8th August, Nixon announced his resignation. It took effect the next day.

On 9th August, Nixon made his tearful, rambling – and sometimes maudlin – farewell to his staff. He insisted to the end that he was innocent of any criminal offences connected with the Watergate scandal. Moreover, he made it clear that he was not leaving the White House a wealthy man. He said wryly: "I only wish I were a wealthy man. At the present time I have to find a way to pay my taxes."

Nixon dismissed the idea that any of his officials had made money. He said: "Sure we've done some things wrong in this administration and the top man always takes the responsibility. But I want to say one thing – no man, or no woman, came into this administration and left it with more of this world's goods than when he came in."

With his voice breaking, Nixon said: "Only if you have been in the deepest valley can you ever know how magnificent it is to be on the highest mountain."

In a final unrepentant gesture, the disgraced president left the White House by helicopter on his way to the Nixon estate in San Clemente, California. Nixon said he wanted to leave the White House as president, and he still was when he took off from Andrews Air Force base just outside Washington in the presidential jet, *The Spirit of '76*. True to his Tricky Dicky image to the last, he bummed a free ride – his powers only running out during the journey when Vice-President Gerald Ford was sworn into office. The ride saved Nixon a few thousand pounds. As a private citizen, he would have had to pay for the journey himself. It was a gesture that did not go unnoticed after his "no climbdown, no guilt, no regrets" resignation speech.

The bugging saga came to end the same day when White House lawyers, acting on behalf of Nixon for the last time, handed a federal judge the last tape. Ford expressed the feelings of the entire nation in his first speech as president: "My fellow Americans, our long national nightmare is over."

However, a month after taking office, Ford stunned America by granting Nixon a "full, free, and absolute pardon" for any offences he may have committed as president, which ended any possibility of an indictment. Ford gave two main reasons for his decision. First, public feeling against Nixon was so strong that it would be impossible for him to get a fair trial in the near future. Second, any delay could threaten Nixon's health and cause even more pain for his family. Nixon was reported to be under strain, and both "absent-minded and terribly depressed". Criticism started almost at once. White House telephone operators reported that immediately after Ford's announcement, "angry calls, heavy and constant" jammed their switchboard. Ford's own press secretary, Jerry terHorst, resigned in protest over the decision, saying it was "a matter of conscience".

In a statement from his San Clemente home, Nixon said of his pardon: "I can see clearly now that I was wrong in not acting more decisively and more forthrightly in dealing with Watergate. No words can describe the depths of my regret and pain at the anguish my mistakes have caused the nation and the presidency. That the way I tried to deal with Watergate was the wrong way is a burden I shall bear for every day of the life that is left to me."

The former president had more cause for thanksgiving when it was reported that he was selling his memoirs for a fat fee. Ford denied there had been any deal between himself and Nixon regarding the pardon, and explained that his decision was taken for the good of the country, not for Nixon's benefit. Ford's controversial decision did move Nixon off the national agenda and allowed the White House administration to focus its resources elsewhere. Nixon's accomplices were charged with criminal offences such as obstruction of justice, misuse of office and lying to federal officials. However, Nixon never underwent a proper trial, as if he was above the law, thus ensuring that the scandal remained a raw wound for the public for decades.

In 1977, British journalist David Frost interviewed Nixon for TV. The interview coincided with the launch of Nixon's memoirs, published by Warner Books, for which he was paid $2.3 million. The interview consisted of four 90-minute shows. Broadcast in 70 countries and watched by 45 million people in America, the show gained the largest audience for a political interview in history. The fact that Nixon made money from his infamy by earning $600,000 for doing the series of interviews – and that he chose to break his silence by teaming up with a foreigner – rankled with some Americans. Nixon admitted his mistakes but denied criminality. He did express regret, saying: "I let the American people down ... I brought myself down."

However, in the interview Nixon made the astounding claim that, as America's president, he was above the law. He told Frost that the president had the power to order burglaries, phone-tapping and other activities that would send the ordinary citizen to jail. Nixon claimed: "When the president does it that means that it is not illegal."

An incredulous Frost asked him if he should have done things through the law rather than add "another crime to the list". Nixon replied: "The proposition you've just stated in theory is perfect. In practice, it just won't work."

In retirement, Nixon attempted to rebuild his reputation, writing several books and undertaking many foreign trips. He suffered a stroke on 18th April 1994, and died four days later at the age of 81. During his presidency, Nixon's best achievements were in foreign policy. He extricated America from the Vietnam War and brought about better relationships with Communist China and the Soviet Union. His efforts as an elder statesman helped to rehabilitate his public image but he never shook off his tainted past. After the Watergate scandal, the use of word "gate" as a suffix entered into popular use to describe a scandal or controversy – it is even listed in the *Oxford English Dictionary*. Its use ensures that it will take time to forget Nixon's ignominious downfall.

As much as the shoddy conduct of royalty and politicians in the pursuit of sex, power and money reflects badly on the institutions they pretend to uphold, the fact that they were questioned, outed and ousted from their positions provides some comfort. Some checks and balances are in place to hold those in positions of power accountable for their actions, and, often, they work. For those accustomed to the pomp, privilege and influence they gain from their positions, losing face, facing justice and enduring public humiliation is the punishment. They may have achieved more than most but they also lost more than most: their place in history is forever besmirched by their weaknesses and failings.

CHAPTER THREE:

LADY LUCK TURNS SOUR

For female stars, the pressures to look good are added to those to perform well again – and again. Life on tour, in the studio and on set can be exhausting. The pursuit of fame and fortune is too much for some: the number to have died young is too large. Film star Lupe "Mexican Spitfire" Vélez died of an overdose of sleeping pills at her home in 1944: she was 34. The glittering shifting hell of Hollywood overwhelmed her. "I see no other way out," she wrote in a suicide note. Actress Carole Landis took an overdose of sleeping tablets in the bathroom of her Hollywood home in 1948. Her career was on the slide. She was 29. Jazz singer Billie Holiday died penniless in 1959, swindled out of her earnings after a life of booze, drug addiction and fighting racial prejudice. She died at the age of 44 of heart and liver disease, and was arrested for drug possession as she lay dying. Rock singer Janis Joplin died in 1970, she was 27. She had just three years of fame – on the last night of her life, she drank a quart of tequila, dosed herself with Valium and pumped a hefty shot of heroin into a vein.

The most famous female star to slide to an early death is the woman whom millions of people throughout the world knew just as "Marilyn". Her wiggle and her wide-eyed look became a legend in her lifetime; in death, she became the ultimate sex goddess and a cultural icon. Actress, singer and model Norma Jeane Mortenson, better known as Marilyn Monroe, was a girl who had washed dishes and worked in a paint-spraying factory before a photographer persuaded her to take off her clothes. What followed from that nude calendar was vintage Hollywood, as she was made into the movie capital's tawdry image. Not long before her death, Monroe said: "Everybody keeps tugging at you. They'd all like a chunk of you. This industry should behave like a mother whose child has just run in front of a car. But instead of clasping the child – they punish it."

Although Monroe came to fame as a sex symbol with dyed blonde curls and a voluptuous figure shown off without underwear, she had a talent for comedy evident in films like 1953's *Gentlemen Prefer Blondes* and 1955's *The Seven-Year Itch*. Monroe craved to be taken seriously as an actress rather than just regarded as a dumb blonde. She studied at New York's prestigious Actors Studio, and the work she put in paid off, winning her awards for roles in 1957's *The Prince and the Showgirl* and 1959's *Some Like It Hot*.

However, Monroe's mood swings caused problems on and off set. Plagued by insomnia, she drove film directors to despair with her nerves and insecurity. She sent frustrated studio heads bellowing to their lawyers. Her use of barbiturates became a problem. Her three failed marriages and affairs with actors, including Marlon Brando, gained her notoriety, while her two miscarriages caused her suffering, as she longed to be a mother. Her legendary status did not end with her death in 1962. Found naked in her Hollywood bungalow, having taken an overdose of barbiturates, Monroe's mode of passing only added to her iconic status. Although ruled as "probable suicide", how she died continues to fascinate: some suggest it was an accidental overdose, some medical malpractice and others murder at the hands of the mob or even the CIA.

Monroe was born in 1926 in Los Angeles, the third child of Gladys Pearl Baker. Her mother was married twice and Monroe biographers suggest that neither husband was Monroe's father. Her mother was mentally unstable and Monroe spent her childhood being passed around: living with family friends, in 10 foster homes and in an orphanage. There is speculation that Monroe was sexually abused as a child while in care, based on her subsequent history of insomnia, substance abuse, suicide attempts and hypersexuality. In *Marilyn Monroe Confidential*, Monroe's maid, Lena Pepitone, wrote that Monroe said she was raped in her early teens by one of her foster parents. Pepitone claimed that Monroe became pregnant as the result of the rape and had a baby boy, whom she was forced to put up for adoption.

The star's itinerant childhood played out in her relationships as an adult. Her three marriages failed. Her first marriage at 16 to Los Angeles cop James Dougherty was a disaster. The second, in 1954, to baseball star Joe

DiMaggio, lasted 10 months. Her third, to playwright Arthur Miller in 1956, was called "a wedding of mind and body" as the King of Broadway made a match with the Queen of Hollywood. It ended in 1961. When that marriage fell apart, Monroe fell apart with it, and nothing, including her psychiatrist, could put her back together again.

Ironically, Monroe's emotional and physical demise accelerated just as she was achieving accolades for her performances. In March 1956, after taking acting lessons with Actors Studio director Lee Strasberg, she went on to play the part of a saloon singer in the romantic comedy, *Bus Stop*. It won her a David di Donatello award – the Italian equivalent of an Oscar. Nevertheless, joy appeared to be a rare luxury for Monroe. Josh Logan, who directed her in *Bus Stop*, said: "I doubt if she had two consecutive days happiness in her entire life."

Monroe had reason to be unhappy. While married to Miller, she lost the baby she had prayed for when she suffered a miscarriage in August 1956. A year later, she had an ectopic pregnancy and attempted to commit suicide. By the time Monroe came to make *Some Like It Hot* in 1958 her behaviour was unpredictable and hostile, she was often a couple of hours late to the set and sometimes refused to leave her dressing room. Monroe suffered from stage fright: before she went on camera, she took deep breaths and flapped her hands – standard relaxing rituals for excruciating nervousness. On *Some Like It Hot*, her perfectionism saw her insist on numerous retakes – as many as 59 takes for one scene. The film won six Academy Award nominations and Monroe a Best Actress Golden Globe award. During filming, Monroe realized she was pregnant. She suffered a second miscarriage in December and made another suicide attempt. Monroe was inconsolable and the bliss of marital life with Miller dissolved swiftly.

In January 1960, Monroe started filming *Let's Make Love*, during which she had an affair with her co-star Yves Montand. The relationship ended badly when Montand refused to leave his wife, actress Simone Signoret. Monroe was in despair. Her insomnia worsened and she increased her use of prescription drugs. Miller attempted to resolve the strain in their marriage, writing a script for a film, *The Misfits*, which included a role for his wife. It was her last film and the shenanigans that took place during production went down in cinematic history. The film cost an unprecedented $3,955,000 and went 40 days over schedule. Shooting began in the Nevada desert in July. Popping Nembutal pills to sleep and drinking too much alcohol made Monroe ill and unable to work. In August, she took an overdose and had her stomach pumped. She had a nervous breakdown and was flown to hospital, where doctors got her off Nembutal, putting her on Dexamyl.

Monroe returned to finish the film but the atmosphere was tense. She rowed with her husband in public and humiliated him. Cast members suffered from the explosive environment and the time spent waiting in the scorching sun for Monroe to turn up on set: Montgomery Clift fell ill and Thelma Ritter ended up in hospital with exhaustion. When filming finished, Miller and Monroe returned to New York on separate flights. Soon after, Monroe announced she and Miller were separating. Worse was to come. Soon after the film was finished, her *The Misfits* co-star Clark Gable died suddenly of a heart attack on the night of 15th November.

Gable respected Monroe and she had looked up to him as a father figure. Reporters contacted Monroe at 2am to tell her the news just hours after he died. Shocked, she became hysterical. Vicious rumours that she killed him upset her. Gable had a weak heart – Monroe's lateness on set and fights with Miller were said to have caused a terrible tension that the actor kept to himself. Monroe started to have awful nightmares. It became impossible for her to sleep without ever-increasing doses of pills.

In January 1961, Monroe's divorce from Miller was finalized. A month later, she had a nervous breakdown and entered the Payne Whitney Psychiatric Clinic in New York. There she wrote a two-page letter to her mentor and friend Lee Strasberg to free her from the psychiatric hospital. Written in a sprawling, childish hand, she pleaded: "I'm locked up with all these poor nutty people. I'm sure to end up a nut if I stay in this nightmare – please help me."

Monroe was terrified of becoming insane because both her grandparents died in asylums and her mother spent years in mental hospitals. Strasberg ignored Monroe's desperate plea, but her ex-husband Joe DiMaggio flew from Florida to New York to obtain her release. In May, Monroe underwent surgery in Los Angeles due to suffering from endometriosis. In June, she was back in hospital again to have her gall bladder removed. By then, she had been in hospital five times in 10 months.

In 1962, Monroe began filming *Something's Got to Give*. On 19th May, during filming, she attended a birthday celebration for President John F. Kennedy at Madison Square Garden, where she sang 'Happy Birthday' for him. She then returned to filming, shooting a sequence in which she appeared nude in a swimming pool – photos of which were released to the press. Despite the sensation the scene caused, 20th Century Fox studio fired Monroe because of her continuous lateness to set, writing off $700,000. Monroe had been physically sick from anxiety about her performance and had been ill with a virus. As the studio filed a lawsuit against her, the world and the press asked if Monroe was finished. Pessimists pointed to her age and the fact her last two films had flopped at the box office. Her health was a problem, too. However, only months earlier, in March, after taking opinion polls in every country where American films are shown, the Hollywood Press Association had announced that Monroe was still the most popular female star in the world.

Monroe resolved the dispute with 20th Century Fox. Her contract was renewed and she was scheduled to recommence filming on *Something's Got to Give* in autumn 1962. She had several new film deals lined up and the offer of a cabaret show in Las Vegas. Monroe is also thought to have been considering a marriage proposal from DiMaggio. The pair had become close again. DiMaggio was concerned about Monroe's well-being and the people she was involved with, and had quit his job with the idea of looking after her. Then, on 5th August, the actress was found dead in bed behind locked doors in her luxury bungalow in Brentwood, Los Angeles. She was clutching a white telephone, still on its hook. On her bedside table, among 30 bottles, was an empty one, which had contained sleeping pills. The star was naked – as she always slept – and covered only by a sheet and blanket. The coroner's officer said: "It looks like suicide."

Los Angeles county coroner, Dr Theodore Curphey, said a "suicide team" would determine whether Monroe's death was accidental or not. Her body was discovered in the middle of the night, but the timeline regarding her death remains intensely disputed. There are claims that Hollywood publicists and doctors were called long before the police and paramedics, who were notified at 4.25am. At the time, it was reported that the housekeeper at Monroe's home, Eunice Murray, woke up at 2am and saw the light on under the star's door. Initially, Murray said that she woke at midnight, but she later retracted this statement. Whatever the truth of the timing, she tried the door and knocked, but could not rouse Monroe. She then called the star's personal physician and psychiatrist, Dr Ralph Greenson, and together they broke into the room. Another doctor, Dr Hyman Engelberg, was also called, but Monroe was dead. It was reported that doctors thought she had died between 8pm and 9pm the previous night. Two days after her death the coroner announced: "Marilyn died from a massive overdose of drugs – nearly twice that needed to kill her."

Later that month, the official inquiry into Monroe's death ended – with a big question mark. The coroner gave his verdict as "probable suicide". However, his "suicide" team of three psychiatrists said that the star might not have intended to die when she took an overdose of drugs. Their report showed that Monroe had tried to kill herself on previous occasions when disappointed or depressed. The psychiatrists said that after each of the earlier attempts she had called for help – and had been saved. They added that the pattern of events leading up to Monroe's death – she was found in bed, clutching a telephone – was the same. Except that this time, rescue never came. The psychiatrists reported: "We have learned that Miss Monroe had often expressed wishes to give up, to withdraw, and even to die. She had suffered from psychiatric disturbance for a long time. She experienced severe fears and frequent depressions."

The coroner said Monroe's death was caused by an overdose of the sedative Nembutal. She had received a prescription for 40 to 50 tablets only three days before her death. The bottle was found empty in her room. DiMaggio made the funeral arrangements and buried his ex-wife on 8th August at the Westwood Village Memorial Park Cemetery in Los Angeles. He restricted the number of mourners, inviting only her closest friends, and refused to invite the Hollywood elite, Frank Sinatra and the Kennedy brothers, whom he felt had let his ex-wife down and were in some way responsible for her decline and death.

There are several theories regarding Monroe's death. Some believe she was murdered, including the first police detective to arrive at the scene, Jack Clemmons from the Los Angeles Police Department. He believed that her room was a staged death scene, accusing LAPD of being involved in a cover-up. Clemmons was replaced and ordered to keep quiet. No murder charges were ever filed. Clemmons said later: "I felt I'd arrived at the scene of a murder. Her body was artfully arranged by someone. It was obvious to me that this was a staged event. Her legs were arranged perfectly, as if she was getting ready to pose for a nude calendar. I had been at suicide scenes before, especially when the victim overdosed on barbiturates. In the last minutes before consciousness is lost, there is great pain and the body contorts."

The detective said that housekeeper Eunice Murray had behaved suspiciously, was evasive when questioned, and was doing laundry at 4.30am on the morning Monroe was found. Murray was installed as housekeeper by Monroe's psychiatrist Ralph Greenson, with instructions to watch over the actress and report any dangerous or suspicious behaviour to him. It has been suggested that Greenson was involved in a cover-up and that either he or Murray had administered a chloral hydrate enema sedative to the actress as part of a treatment to wean her off barbiturates. The enema then reacted fatally with the Nembutal pills Monroe had taken, which had been prescribed by Dr Hyman Engelberg. If so, that would explain Murray's evasiveness, as the actress may have died because of tragic medical error. Most of the documents pertaining to Greenson's treatment of Monroe have been sealed until 2039.

Documents and items were also found to have been removed from Monroe's home, including her red diary and the contents of her filing cabinet. Over the years, it has become clear that Monroe had fallen head over heels in love with the married President John F. Kennedy, but that he had passed her on to his brother, Bobby. In *Marilyn: At Rainbow's End: Sex, Lies, Murder and the Great Cover-Up*, author Darwin Porter – who knew the star – claims that Attorney General Bobby promised to leave his wife for Monroe, but weeks before she died he stopped returning her calls. Distraught, Marilyn had a brief fling with the youngest Kennedy brother, Ted, then started telling friends she was going to call a press conference to reveal all her affairs. She told pals she was pregnant but was not sure whether the father was the president or Bobby. Porter asserts that Bobby secretly visited Monroe with his brother-in-law Peter Lawford hours before she died, perhaps to tell her that the affair was finished – which, if true, may explain why she felt suicidal. Porter also speculates that the mafia killed Monroe by administering the enema on someone's orders. The author posits that Monroe became entangled with the mob after bedding mafia boss Sam Giancana's henchman, Johnny Roselli, and that Monroe intended to expose the mafia's secrets too.

The ongoing debate about Monroe's death keeps her iconic status alive. She did have problems, crazy moods and intense frustrations everyday people do not have to deal with. But friends also point out she had a good heart, a terrific sense of humour and the kindest understanding of other people's troubles. Her talent as an actress has achieved greater recognition in the years since her death than when she was alive – and that is perhaps how she would have wanted to be remembered.

Hollywood success was what damaged Judy Garland early in life. She made the transition from child star in musicals to an Oscar-nominated serious dramatic actress. Yet Garland is best known for her contralto voice and the vicissitudes of her career, which were as dramatic as any role she played. Success took its toll on her health mentally and physically, as she came apart in a welter of booze, pills and suicide attempts. She collapsed in the studios. She collapsed on the theatre stage. She saw psychiatrists and received controversial electroconvulsive therapy. There were serious illnesses, long recoveries, disasters of forgotten lyrics, drink-fuddled lyrics, boos at first nights and bravoes at triumphant comebacks.

Born into a vaudeville family as Frances Gumm in 1922 in Minnesota, Garland joined her two sisters in a song and dance troupe, The Gumm

Sisters. Garland's story followed a familiar Hollywood pattern. First, came the luck – the day in 1934 when she walked into the vast Metro-Goldwyn-Mayer studios as an unknown 12-year-old, asked for a job and got it. Garland won over America with her films *Every Sunday Afternoon* made in 1935 and *Broadway Melody of 1938*. Then, in 1939, came the picture that made her one of Tinseltown's great money-spinners, *The Wizard of Oz*. In it, she sang 'Over the Rainbow', a song she was still being asked to sing nearly 30 years later. A Special Academy Award in 1940 for her outstanding performance as a screen juvenile crowned her success. Garland was a world star at 17.

However, Garland's was a pressure-cooked adolescent stardom. The effects of that stayed with her for the rest of her life. Garland's appearance did not measure up to cinematic glamour. She had to have her teeth capped and wear rubber discs to reshape her nose, and the insinuation that she was an ugly duckling left her feeling insecure. The studio gave her amphetamines to curb her appetite in order to keep her slim – if she gained weight, she could be suspended without pay – and barbiturates before bed to make her sleep, laying the foundation for her subsequent dependency. Garland said later: "I missed the gentle maturing most girls have. I was born at the age of twelve on a Metro-Goldwyn-Mayer lot."

As Garland worked on films that earned an estimated £25 million for MGM, she began to pay the price for her success. She was working to exhaustion point – and beyond. In late July 1947, after filming *The Pirate*, Garland made her first suicide attempt. She had been off sick on several occasions throughout filming as she struggled with her dependence on prescription medicines, and finally had a nervous breakdown, cutting her wrists with broken glass. The star was admitted to a sanitarium in California and then a psychiatric hospital in Massachusetts. By September, she was back in rehearsals for *Easter Parade*. It was the last big musical she made for MGM.

In June 1948, Garland began rehearsals on *The Barkleys of Broadway*, but the strain of successive projects had left her frail. She was taking prescription sleeping pills and illicitly obtained tablets containing morphine. She began to develop a drinking problem. Suffering from migraines, she missed several days of filming and MGM suspended her from the film in July. In March 1949, she began work on *Annie Get Your Gun* but was suspended two months later for failing to turn up at shoots. Garland went to Peter Bent Brigham Hospital in Boston in an attempt to cure her addiction to prescription drugs, and later returned to MGM, completing *Summer Stock* in March 1950.

Garland began filming on *Royal Wedding*, but, on 17th June, she was suspended for failing to appear for work. Two days later, Garland made a second suicide attempt, scratching her throat in a cry for help. MGM said the star made a wound in her throat with a piece of glass "in a fit of anguish". An MGM spokesman said: "Miss Garland became very despondent and hysterical and rushed to the bathroom, locking the door. She broke a drinking glass and then made the wound. Her husband got her to open the door and immediately she was very repentant."

In September, MGM agreed to Garland's request to be released from her contract. Her so-called "concert years" then began. The studios may have been tired of Garland but her fans were not. In October 1951, she took to Broadway for 19 weeks and triumphed. She returned to the big screen in 1954. The press announced: "At thirty-one, Judy Garland is back: the old Judy – the slim, smiling, happy singing star everyone loved in such gay films as *The Wizard of Oz* … the first still to be released from her 'comeback' film, *A Star is Born* … shows that after four years away from the screen Judy has at last lost the weight that started the rows with the Metro-Goldwyn-Mayer studio. Judy, the girl who became plump, turned to the stage after she had a nervous breakdown. But now Warner Brothers have brought her back to films." The film garnered critical plaudits but lost money. What audiences did not know is that Garland had pleaded illness during filming, just as she had done at MGM.

In November 1959, she was hospitalized and diagnosed with acute hepatitis. Over the next seven weeks, several quarts of fluid were drained from her body. Doctors told her she would not sing again and that she had five years or less to live. This time she was prescribed Valium, Thorazine and Ritalin. To make matters worse, she owed the taxman and was in financial difficulties. However, the feisty star rallied. She went on to tour and made more films, including 1961's acclaimed *Judgment at Nuremberg*, which won Garland an Oscar nomination.

Garland's domestic life was as stormy as her career. She just could not have a love affair without getting married. Her first husband was composer David Rose – married 1941, divorced 1944. Next came director Vincente Minnelli – married 1945, divorced 1951. For the next 13 years, she was married to producer Sid Luft. After their divorce in 1965, she married actor

Mark Herron – and divorced him two years later. In 1969, the year of her death, she married the much younger Mickey Deans, a businessman.

The star's divorce from Luft saw her dirty laundry aired when the couple fought over the custody of their two young children, Lorna and Joe. In the spring of 1962, the battle was in full flow with Luft threatening proceedings to take them away. Luft claimed that two men held him in his hotel room in New York while Garland took a plane to London where she was due to film *The Lonely Stage*. She took their children with her, claiming Luft had threatened to take them from her and tried to declare her an "unfit mother". When she arrived in Britain in May, she hired a bodyguard for the children and later had them made wards of court. After this, in October 1964, Luft went to court to seek custody of his children. Garland's former agent, Vernon Alves, told the court that after Garland appeared at a show in Philadelphia in May 1961, she ran from room to room in a hotel without any clothes on and then tried to jump from a window. Alves said that Garland began drinking in the hotel: "[She] kicked at a TV set and behaved in a manner that terrified me. I spent most of my time trying to catch her and she was bouncing off the walls. The last thing I did was catch her before she could get out of the window."

Alves said that, shortly afterwards, Garland dismissed him. Garland's former housekeeper revealed that the star had appeared intoxicated in front of her children "many times", saying: "She would speak to them in a loud and intoxicated voice."

The housekeeper added that every day she carried empty bottles out of Garland's bedroom and that the maid carried in full ones. Garland's former hairdresser said that on a 1961 concert tour the singer would "pack a basket containing her personal belongings, four bottles of white wine and an ice bucket". Garland alleged Luft struck her "many times". Luft was granted joint custody and the couple divorced in May 1965.

Garland drank because she was scared. She drank because of a conviction that it helped her over the first testing moments of a show. When the alcohol proved to be no panacea, she took to an assortment of pills and stimulants, buying courage to face the dawn, for she was terrified by the nights and slept fitfully during the day. In the last few years of Garland's life, she performed on quicksand. The more she struggled to regain the heights, the further she slipped. In the turmoil of her private life writ followed writ: court actions were threatened then settled. Sometimes she was wronged, and sometimes she just forgot to pay bills and overlooked the fine print in her contracts. Those who watched her perform were as fascinated as a circus audience looking at the act on the high wire – and Garland knew that, joking: "They think I'm worried about falling. What they don't realise is I'm playing Russian roulette."

On 30th May 1965, when Garland played Cincinnati, Ohio, hundreds of fans besieged the singer in her dressing room shouting for their money back after she stopped in the middle of her show. Garland began the concert to a warm welcome from the audience of 4,000. After six or seven songs, she said there would be an intermission. Half an hour later, the audience was told there were "some problems" but the show would continue. Forty-five minutes later, Garland walked on stage with her doctor. She said she was ill and that her doctor had decided she could not continue because she had a virus infection. The announcement started a rumpus that lasted two hours, and a box-office window was broken in the uproar. Eventually, six policemen escorted Garland to her car and she returned to her hotel.

In February 1967, Garland planned to make yet another comeback film, *Valley of the Dolls*. Her role was that of a tough, ageing musical star – a daring parallel to reality. She missed rehearsals during filming and, in April, stalked from the set after a row with studio bosses.

In early January 1969, Garland started a five-week run at London's Talk of the Town. She married Mickey Deans on 9th January at a private ceremony at a chapel in London during her Talk of the Town residency. However, the legality of the marriage was in doubt because her divorce papers to her fourth husband, Mark Herron, were not finalized until 11th February.

The Talk of the Town engagement was not an entire success: Garland was a walking casualty as she tripped over the microphone lead, struggled with a shoulder strap and caught a stiletto heel in her long feather boa. Her singing fell short of its legendary quality. She sang badly and with panic. On some occasions, she got a stormy reception – including boos and a barrage of bread rolls. Deans said she had flu.

While still starring at Talk of the Town, Garland appeared on TV in *The London Palladium Show* on 19th January. Her 10-minute star spot on the show went wrong from the start. The compère, comedian Jimmy Tarbuck, introduced her but she did not appear on stage for nearly two minutes. Towards the end of the act, Garland seemed to have trouble pronouncing the words of towns in a song about Britain. She bent down and asked the orchestra how the lyrics went. At the end of her spot, she threw her arms round Tarbuck, who helped her on to the Palladium "roundabout". A show spokesman said the singer was suffering from flu.

Garland and Deans married in a legal ceremony on 15th March at Chelsea Registry Office. On their honeymoon, in Torremolinos in Spain, she became seriously ill. For five days, she could not leave her hotel room. The couple returned to their home at Cadogan Lane in London's Chelsea.

Garland died on 22nd June 1969. The 47-year-old star was found dead at her home in Chelsea. Deans discovered her body in the toilet after he woke up. At the time of her death a Harley Street surgeon told the *Daily Mirror*: "I examined Judy eight years ago and discovered she had cirrhosis of the liver. I read her the riot act. I told her to knock off the booze or it was curtains. She must have been a good girl because when I examined her two years ago she was improved. But she was on borrowed time. Quite honestly, she lived three years longer than was forecast. Judy was a great fighter, a great person and she knew it would be the end a long time ago if she paid no heed to the warnings."

At the inquest held later that month the coroner said Garland had died of barbiturate poisoning due to an "incautious self-overdose". Deans described her last hours, saying they decided to watch TV instead of going to the theatre. Just after midnight they went to bed: "Before going to sleep, Judy curled her feet up to me to keep warm, as she always did," he said.

Next morning, the telephone woke him. It was someone for Garland. She was not in bed, so Deans looked round the house and found the bathroom door locked. He thought there was nothing strange about her locking the bathroom door. It dated back to her film days when, as a girl standing in a slip with men walking around her, she felt self-conscious. He looked through the bathroom window when he got no reply and saw Garland slumped, as if asleep. He climbed in. "As I picked her up I thought she moaned," he said. Deans then called the police.

The pathologist said that a post-mortem examination revealed some superficial and old cuts on the front of the singer's wrists, which seemed to be self-inflicted. There was a high barbiturate level in her bloodstream, sufficient to cause death. A small amount of alcohol was also present. It appeared that the tablets had been taken over a period of time. Garland may have taken another dose while only half under the influence of a previous dose, because the effects wore off so quickly. The pathologist estimated that she had taken 10 1½-grain tablets, and said that death was due to barbiturate poisoning. He found no sign of cirrhosis of the liver and no effects of chronic alcoholism. The examination showed that she had not taken a single massive dose of barbiturates, but had been in the habit of taking them regularly, so that the level in the blood was high.

Garland's doctor said that she had difficulty in eating and suffered mood fluctuations, suffering occasional bouts of depression. He said that she did not drink a great deal: "She would have a vodka, mix it with fruit juices, and merely sip it. I have seen her do this for one or two hours."

The coroner stated that there was no evidence to suggest the tragedy was a deliberate act on the part of Garland and there was no question of alcoholism. The evidence gave a clear picture of a person who had been habituated to barbiturates for a long time.

In death, Garland has iconic status, her young face imprinted forever in many people's hearts as that of the innocent and vivacious Dorothy Gale in *The Wizard of Oz*. However, the gruelling pace of work she endured as a teenage star and the studio's cavalier treatment of a valuable asset damaged her irreparably, both physically and emotionally. Ever the gutsy trouper, she continued to perform even when her body and her voice were failing her. At her best, fans found her incomparable, at her worst they usually forgave her. She remains revered as one of the 20th century's greatest entertainers.

The demise of divas, singers and film stars in the 20th century made news. Yet, when a new century arrived, their heartbreaking stories did not prevent others from following in their footsteps. Singer Amy Winehouse died at 27 – the same age as Brian Jones, Jimi Hendrix, Janis Joplin and Jim Morrison – ensuring that the skinny Londoner with a vertiginous beehive hairdo joined music's rock martyrs. Winehouse exploded on to the music scene in the early years of the 21st century, yet her music seemed steeped in the music of the ages. She loved the soul, jazz and funk of black America and, despite being a working-class Jewish girl from north London, her smoky faultless voice drew comparisons with America's greatest jazz singers. Winehouse was a songwriter of dazzling originality and a charismatic performer. As an individual, she was said to be fun, witty, vivacious and big-hearted. However, her journey to self-destruction was talked about as much as her musical talent during her short life.

The daughter of a London cab driver and jazz fan, Mitch, and a pharmacist, Janis, Winehouse grew up wanting to do nothing but make music. She achieved her goal, won numerous awards and sold millions of albums. However, the obsessive personality that helped make her a superb songwriter came with flaws that affected her personal life and well-being. Winehouse would veer from gorging on bags of fizzy sweets to going for days at a time without eating – she went on whisky benders, and had self-harming episodes, a sunbed obsession and, eventually, a drug addiction. When the drugs took their insidious hold on her, she could be belligerent and bad-tempered. The paparazzi managed to capture various outbursts on film, making for what must be one of the most public tragic downfalls of modern times.

Winehouse recorded her first album *Frank* when she was just 19. Her sultry voice and soulful lyrics made it a hit when it debuted in 2003. As the young singer's popularity grew, inevitably her life off-stage began to attract attention. In October 2004, she was snapped getting drunk and "stumbling all over the place" at London's 10 Room nightclub. In 2005, she dated music-video production assistant Blake Fielder-Civil, then fell into depression after they split up. Winehouse's drinking escalated: her favourite tipple was a Rickstasy cocktail – three parts vodka, one part Baileys, banana liqueur and Southern Comfort. Her behaviour caused panic among aides as she turned up to interviews and TV appearances late and drunk. The singer's bosses at Island Records told her to cut back on her drinking or go into rehab. She once got as far as the reception desk at a rehab clinic – an episode that formed the basis of her 2006 hit single, 'Rehab'. Later, Winehouse recalled: "Yes, things got so bad for me at one point that I was told: 'We're taking you to rehab and, if you don't come today, we're taking you tomorrow.' So I went and this guy behind the desk tells me that I have to fill out some long-winded form. The questions were about how much I drink, that kind of thing. So I was like, how long is it going to take? He said about half an hour and that was too much. The only reason I was drinking was because I was depressed over a break-up. It didn't go deeper than that. I don't ever want to be one of those people who can't be around drink. I can drink a lot, have a good time and not be absolutely tw*tted. It's fun. But the problem is that if you do it every night, you just wear yourself out."

A low point came in October 2006, when Winehouse appeared on Charlotte Church's TV chat show. Before going on the programme, Winehouse had been drinking heavily: she had drunk champagne for breakfast and then had a lunch of vodka, whisky, Baileys and liqueurs. She also hit the bar at the TV studio. By the time Winehouse got in front of the cameras she was bleary-eyed and slurring her words. It took three attempts for her to record a duet of Michael Jackson's 'Beat It' with stunned host Church. With the release of Winehouse's second album, *Back to Black*, the same month, the singer's pain emerged. Inspired by her break-up with Fielder-Civil, her agony was evident in her song lyrics.

The once voluptuous star set tongues wagging when she made her comeback looking gaunt and painfully thin. Pictures of her thin figure led to whispers that she was suffering from an eating disorder. In January 2007, she stumbled off stage at London's GAY nightclub after just one song. Organizers blamed food poisoning but most put it down to yet another untimely booze bender. However, the public and the critics loved Winehouse's music, and she gained Brit Awards nominations for Best

Female Solo Artist and Best British Album. In February, in an interview with the *Daily Mirror* on the eve of the awards ceremony, she appeared to be happier, and by then had a new boyfriend, chef Alex Clare. She explained her rapid weight loss, saying: "I lost the weight when I stopped smoking weed and started working out. I used to smoke £200 of pot a week – which is disgusting – and it made me eat junk. Now I think that going to the gym is the best drug. I go four times a week and it gives me the buzz I need."

Winehouse said she did not even notice losing the weight: "A lot was made of it and, for about a nanosecond, I went through a phase where I wouldn't eat. I sometimes joke that I woke up in the morning and decided to be anorexic but by 2pm, I'd changed my mind. Some people reckoned that I looked healthier when I was bigger but I had terrible skin and no energy. Anyway, I've recently put on 7lbs."

In what proved to be a poignant statement highlighting her binge drinking, Winehouse said she might have finally worked out how to manage her partying: "My new thing is to try to do one night on, one night off."

Winehouse went on to win the coveted gong for Best British Female Solo Artist. Her success proved that, despite a year of being snapped falling out of nightclubs after drunken nights on the town, she still had what it takes as a musician. In March, Winehouse was back in the press after a brief split with her boyfriend, Clare, that led to the distraught singer going on a booze bender and cancelling two gigs at Shepherd's Bush Empire. The same month, Winehouse told *Q Magazine* that she still suffered bouts of depression – and ended up "slapping herself". "Not punching myself in the face, but slapping," she said. "I drank a whole bottle of champagne and then just got depressed. I didn't feel like I looked good. And I'm quite self-destructive when I'm drunk."

The star admitted she found the pain of having 13 tattoos "relieving". She said: "It's a way of suffering for the things that mean a lot to you. Actually, I like the pain. To me, it relieves you."

Winehouse's relationship with Clare ended when she got back together with Fielder-Civil. Often described as "soul mates", the couple were engaged in April and were married the following month in Miami Beach, Florida. Friends were said to be "stunned" because Winehouse – who had Fielder-Civil's name tattooed above her left breast – had been heartbroken when he previously cheated on her, inspiring the dark lyrics on *Back to Black*.

Soon it became obvious what a terrible idea the couple's reunion was: Winehouse's husband was the person who first persuaded her to try heroin. Only two weeks after they tied the knot, Winehouse caused a stir when she arrived at the MTV Movie Awards in Los Angeles. Onlookers said she was unsteady on her feet as she walked up the red carpet, resting her head on her husband's shoulder. Visibly jittery, she sang 'Rehab' but jeers from the crowd left her upset, and later she was photographed having an argument with her husband on the street. In August, it was evident that the pace of touring, combined with her drinking, was taking its toll. Winehouse cancelled a series of scheduled performances, citing exhaustion. After a three-day bender, indulging in a cocktail of cocaine, ketamine, ecstasy, vodka and whisky, she collapsed at home. Her husband rushed her to hospital with a drugs overdose and she had her stomach pumped.

Afterwards, Winehouse checked into The Priory rehab centre in London.

Family members admitted that her relentless drink-and-drug lifestyle had pushed her to the brink. Winehouse's worried father-in-law, Lance Fielder, blamed her breakdown on massive booze and drugs binges. He dismissed her record company's excuse of "severe exhaustion" as a "cover-up", saying Fielder-Civil had spoken to him about his concerns: "He told me he was very worried about her. He admitted they both drank and did drugs but that came as no surprise. It was brought on by all her excesses. Yes, work is one of them, but there's the drink and drugs too. She's got to get a grip on herself before it's too late."

However, the singer fled The Priory after just one night. Her worried father Mitch called a family summit to sort out her problems at the Four Seasons Hotel in Hook, Hampshire, paid for by the star's record company. After an emotional showdown with their families, Winehouse and her husband admitted they needed help, and that she was addicted to heroin and cocaine. They went into drug rehab at the £10,000-a-week Causeway Retreat, set on a private island off the Essex coast. Yet the couple's stay was brief: after just five days, they abandoned the clinic by helicopter. Their families were horrified by the couple's decision to quit treatment, which was expected to last six to eight weeks. The pair were supposed to discuss their problems at a crucial meeting with doctors after they left the treatment clinic. However, Winehouse never turned up and was spotted in a pub near her home in Camden, north London. Her touring commitments were put on hold until September while Winehouse and her husband agreed to return to the clinic.

Winehouse's mother, Janis, who separated from her father when their

"FATTY" ARBUCKLE ON HIS TRIAL: FIRST PICTURES

LEFT: The first trial of comedian and silent movie star Roscoe "Fatty" Arbuckle on the charge of manslaughter made front-page news in 1921.

BELOW: A large crowd gathered to see off the flower-covered casket containing the body of Virginia Rappe as it was placed in the hearse for her funeral in Hollywood in 1921. The starlet's death was the basis of the manslaughter charge against Roscoe "Fatty" Arbuckle.

LEFT: "It Girl" Clara Bow attended the trial of her former secretary, Daisy DeVoe (inset), in Los Angeles in 1931. Bow wept during the hearing.

RIGHT: Movie star Clara Bow in court being questioned during the 1931 trial of her former secretary, Daisy DeVoe, on charges of stealing money, clothing and jewellery from her.

BELOW: A crowd of people huddle round a radio to listen to the abdication speech of King Edward VIII on 11th December 1936. His abdication shocked the nation and the world.

ABOVE: Edward, Duke of Windsor, and his wife, Wallis, Duchess of Windsor, during the Second World War. The duke was desperate for a role in the war effort but the British government sidelined the former monarch, possibly unhappy with the couple's closeness to fascists before the war.

RIGHT: Conservative Party minister John Profumo and wife, actress Valerie Hobson, pictured in about 1961 before the scandal known as the Profumo affair brought about his resignation in 1963.

ABOVE: The woman at the centre of the Profumo affair: Christine Keeler returning to her flat in Devonshire Street, London, after visiting the police on 20ᵗʰ June 1963.

ABOVE: Former government minister John Stonehouse was found alive in Australia in December 1974 after faking his own death.

RIGHT: Runaway MP John Stonehouse goes to jail in 1976 for fraud, theft and forgery.

LEFT: Lord Lambton quit his job as a government minister in May 1973 after he was snapped in bed with prostitutes.

BELOW: Disgraced former MP Lord Lambton smoked cannabis and used to talk about drugs while in bed with call girl Norma Levy.

BELOW: President Richard Nixon waves to the crowds from Air Force One with his wife Pat as they arrive for a tour of Ireland in 1970, two years before the Watergate burglary that led to his downfall.

RIGHT: President Richard Nixon boards a helicopter to leave the White House after his resignation in 1974.

LEFT: Blonde and curvaceous, Marilyn Monroe became the ultimate female sex symbol, yet she yearned to be taken seriously as an actress.

BELOW: Marilyn Monroe arm in arm with her third husband, playwright Arthur Miller, in July 1956.

LEFT: Judy Garland in August 1962 when she battled with her third husband, Sid Luft, regarding their two children.

RIGHT: Judy Garland at the Talk of the Town in London in January 1969. A poor performance saw the singer struggling through her signature song, 'Over the Rainbow'. The audience pelted the star with bread sticks and cigarette butts.

RIGHT: Amy Winehouse arriving at London's Holborn police station in April 2008 after being invited in for questioning. The troubled singer was accused of head-butting a member of the public during an incident.

LEFT: Singer Amy Winehouse performing at the V Festival at Hylands Park, Chelmsford in August 2008.

ABOVE: Whitney Houston in concert at Earls Court Exhibition Centre, London in November 1993 during The Bodyguard World Tour when her fame was at its height.

LEFT: Singer Whitney Houston arriving with her entourage at Glasgow Airport in April 2010.

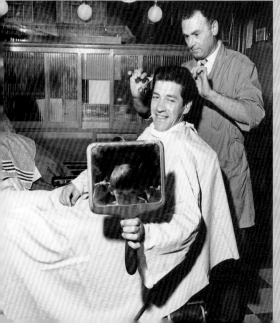

ABOVE: The King of Rock: Elvis Presley signing autographs while in Germany on service with the US army in the late 1950s. He began abusing prescription drugs while stationed in Germany.

OPPOSITE: King of Pop Michael Jackson in March 2009 at the O2 Arena in London. He unveiled plans for his comeback gigs and told screaming fans: "When I say this is it, this really is it ... the final curtain call."

LEFT: Michael Holliday, known as Britain's Bing Crosby, at the barber's in June 1960.

KING OF POP
MICHAEL
JACKSON
THIS IS IT

MICHAELJACKSONLIVE.COM

ABOVE: Rolling Stones guitarist Brian Jones sneaks into a Harley Street nursing home in December 1967 after avoiding a prison sentence.

LEFT: Brian Jones with model Donyale Luna at the filming of the Rolling Stones Rock 'n' Roll Circus in December 1968. It turned out to be his final public appearance with the band.

ABOVE: Sid Vicious of punk band the Sex Pistols in May 1978 as he tries to assault a photographer.

RIGHT: Punk rocker Sid Vicious of the Sex Pistols injects himself with heroin in 1978. Within the year, he was dead from a drugs overdose.

LEFT: Thin Lizzy frontman Phil Lynott on stage playing guitar in 1977.

BELOW: Thin Lizzy singer and guitarist Phil Lynott struggled to beat his drug addiction, but eventually it killed him.

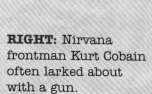

LEFT: Singer, guitarist and songwriter Kurt Cobain helped to make grunge music mainstream.

RIGHT: Nirvana frontman Kurt Cobain often larked about with a gun.

ABOVE: Newspaper baron Robert Maxwell pictured with Prime Minister Margaret Thatcher in 1985. Success and wealth gave the crooked tycoon access to the corridors of power.

BELOW: Derby County management and players go down on their knees to acclaim benefactor Robert Maxwell after the team was promoted to League Division One in May 1987.

ABOVE: TV presenter, DJ and child molester Jimmy Savile on the set of the BBC's *Top of the Pops* show in October 1971.

daughter was nine, told the *Daily Mirror* of her heartache: "Her father warned her he would do whatever it took. She said she'd only go if she could go with Blake. It was at least a start."

She continued: "I don't even think this is Amy's fault. I think her brain's addled. This isn't Amy. It's as if her whole life has turned into a stage performance." Janis revealed her daughter had always been reckless and once predicted she would die young, saying: "I don't think I'm going to survive that long."

Janis went on: "A part of me has prepared myself for this over the years. It's as though she's created her own ending. She's on a path of self-mutilation, quite literally. What else are all the tattoos about? I hate them. They're horrible. It's like a sickness but she cannot see it."

She blamed her daughter's troubles on entering the record industry too young and being unable to cope with her staggering success. But as Winehouse's star began to rise, she and Janis drifted apart. "To begin with, after she left home, she would ring me every day," said Janis. "Then, once she started travelling more, I started to feel a detachment. I think she was too young. She lacks the maturity to cope."

Janis added: "For most of her life, I've been aware of needing to keep an eye on her. She's reckless. No one can stop her once she's made her mind up but she never thinks of the consequences."

At first, Janis thought her daughter only had problems with alcohol and had no idea about her eating disorders or self-harming. She said: "Last summer she performed at a friend's wedding and was sick in the loos. Then, before Christmas, she admitted she had anorexia and bulimia.

Her self-harming was never apparent."

Janis' fears came true when Winehouse and Fielder-Civil quit the rehab clinic for a second time later that month. Just when it appeared things couldn't get any worse for the troubled star, life took another dreadful turn. Only hours after she was nominated for four MOBO Awards, Winehouse fled down London's Regent Street, and Fielder-Civil was spotted frantically searching for her, stopping random members of the public and asking if they had seen his wife. Eventually, the couple caught up with each other. They returned to London's Sanderson Hotel, where they were staying, shortly before 5am. Winehouse arrived at the hotel with her arm covered in bandages, blood seeping from a large gash in her knee, bloodstained shoes and mascara streaming down her face. Her husband was in an even worse state, with large slashes to his face and neck and what witnesses said appeared to be the letter "A" carved into his cheeks.

Winehouse's appearance was so shocking that a stunned hotel worker called the police. Police interviewed the singer at the hotel but she convinced them that everything was fine. After hearing the news, her father Mitch dashed to the hotel where he held a five-hour crisis talk with his daughter in the bar. Later, Winehouse sensationally confessed to the press to self-harming before attempting to take drugs with a prostitute. She leapt to the defence of her husband, claiming he "saved her life" after catching her cutting herself and stepping in to stop her. Winehouse also admitted she was responsible for her husband's savaged face after the pair of them turned up bruised and bloody at the hotel.

The couple then packed up and moved to the nearby Covent Garden

Hotel – but their erratic behaviour disturbed guests and so they left early, escaping to Saint Lucia for a holiday. Then, a bitter family row exploded. In a Radio 5 Live interview, Fielder-Civil's mother and stepfather accused Winehouse's record label of failing to help conquer her drug problem and called on fans to stop buying her records. However, Winehouse's father claimed the families were pulling in different directions and said her record chiefs did care. The hellish summer continued when reports emerged that Winehouse was sick over a sofa as she sat drinking in the only restaurant at the exclusive Jade Mountain resort in Saint Lucia – sparking new fears for her health. The stench was so bad the hotel was forced to shut while it was cleaned. Winehouse also violently vomited blood in her hotel room. Maids sent to clean the £700-a-night suite were "horrified" by the mess. One worker revealed: "There was blood and vomit all over the bathroom, it was just terrible. It looked like she'd been sick many times. There was blood mixed up in the vomit. It was sickening ... The hotel management offered to send for a doctor but Amy declined. She said she'd be fine. Everyone was concerned because she looked so frail."

Ironically, Winehouse's troubles only increased demand for her music. In July, the singer sold 88,273 albums and by the end of August she had sold 102,084. The scandal surrounding the artist had sent sales sky-high. When Winehouse returned to Britain, she announced she was back at work on a new album, insisting: "I'm sorted out. Nothing's wrong with me." After downing vodka cocktails at her birthday party at London's Century Club, she vowed never to return to rehab, saying: "I didn't enjoy it and don't want to go back. I missed my friends and my parents. I have been doing better now and that's because of my friends."

In October, while on European tour, Winehouse spoke to German magazine *Stern* about the overdose that had nearly killed her, saying: "I saw a picture of myself when I came out of the hospital. I didn't recognise myself. Since I was sixteen, I've felt a black cloud hangs over me. Since then, I have taken pills for depression." Her comments came just days after she spent a night in a cell in Norway for possessing cannabis; she was fined £350 and released.

The next month, Winehouse won the Artists' Choice gong at the MTV Europe Awards. However, her husband's arrest overshadowed the joy of receiving the award. Fielder-Civil and a friend were due to stand trial charged with assaulting a barman the previous year; however, they were now alleged to have offered him £200,000, plus £10,000 costs, to change his story and go to Spain until the case collapsed. Winehouse could not cope with the stress and, in a string of shambolic shows, fans booed the distressed singer. A doctor at a London clinic advised her to cancel all appearances and she pulled out of her UK tour to seek help for her drug addiction. She said: "I can't give it my all on stage without my Blake. I'm so sorry but I don't want to do the shows half-heartedly. I love singing but my husband is everything to me and without him it's not the same."

Winehouse brushed with the law in May 2008 when she was arrested over a video showing her allegedly smoking crack cocaine. No charges were brought. When her husband's case went to trial in July, he pleaded guilty and was sentenced to jail for 27 months. Winehouse's behaviour became erratic and the fragile star was reported to have lashed out at fans on more than one occasion. Her parents attempted to aid her as she unravelled, and Mitch suggested she should be sectioned. Winehouse started taking drug replacements in August.

In November, Fielder-Civil gained early release from jail to enter rehab. The evening he was released Winehouse was involved in a bust-up with photographers outside her home in Camden. She launched herself at a crowd of paparazzi, screaming: "Who's first – who wants some?" The star threw her bag on the ground before throwing punches and trying to grab their cameras. A month later, Fielder-Civil was sent back to prison after breaching his bail conditions.

In an effort to quit drugs, Winehouse went to Saint Lucia for a two-month break. When she returned to England in early 2009 she appeared determined to change her life – and divorce her husband. In May, Winehouse addressed unwelcome paparazzi attention by seeking and gaining a court injunction to prevent them harassing her. In July, she was cleared of charges of assaulting a dancer. A month later, her divorce from Fielder-Civil was finalized. That summer, Mitch revealed that his daughter had been clean of drugs since Christmas. He revealed a remarkable reversal of fortunes, and how the previous summer his daughter had been in a terrible state and, at times, incapable of leaving her bedroom. He said: "She was claustrophobic, agoraphobic. Phobic of everyone and everybody. People were even throwing drugs over the fence and up to her window for her. Until we brought in our own security, we were finding it a difficult situation to resolve."

However, during the star's stay in Saint Lucia her drinking escalated.

Her father insisted: "She doesn't drink all the time, but when she does it's sometimes to excess. I think potentially she could have a drink problem as addicts tend to replace one addiction with another. Her tipple of choice is Jack Daniel's and Coke and when she and her friends get together she can drink too much. But she tells me it's something she will stop – and I believe her. She did it with drugs, so she can do it with alcohol."

He added: "Nine months ago she wasn't coherent. But now she doesn't binge on chocolate like she used to. She's no longer bulimic. She's healthy."

Although clean of drugs, Winehouse's drinking proved to be a problem. Later that year she got into trouble for a foul-mouthed attack on a theatre manager after a booze-fuelled afternoon at a Christmas pantomime. The singer drank five vodka and Cokes while watching a friend perform in *Cinderella* at the Milton Keynes Theatre in Buckinghamshire. Winehouse wanted another double vodka at the bar, but the theatre manager suggested she should have water. The singer then went to the toilet but her four-letter outburst could be heard from outside. The manager asked her to leave and she shouted, "Who the fuck do you think you are?" before pulling the manager's hair. Winehouse's security staff then stepped in to calm the situation. In January 2010, she appeared in court where her lawyer said she had apologized profusely and reiterated her apology. Winehouse admitted common assault and disorderly behaviour. She was given a two-year conditional discharge and was ordered to pay costs and compensation.

By then, Winehouse did appear to be healthier and happier. She had started dating a new man, film director Reg Traviss. She battled hard to conquer her problems with alcohol but was not always successful. In June 2011, she stumbled around the stage during a concert in Belgrade, Serbia, where she was booed off after slurring through songs. The Serbian gig led to her series of European concerts being cancelled. Five weeks later, Winehouse performed for the last time when she joined her goddaughter, Dionne Bromfield, on stage at the Camden Roundhouse.

On 23rd July 2011, Winehouse was found dead at her home in Camden. The police treated her death as unexplained, amid speculation that she died after taking a cocktail of lethal Class A drugs, including a "bad" ecstasy pill. In fact, the singer had no illegal drugs in her system when she died. Police found three empty vodka bottles in her bedroom and an inquest recorded a verdict of death by misadventure after accidental alcohol poisoning: she was five times over the drink-drive limit. She died after a three-day bender, following weeks of abstinence.

The frail, five-times Grammy award winner was due to release her third album in 2010. However, unwilling to produce a less than perfect record, the release date was pushed back repeatedly. When Winehouse died, she left material recorded and ready to be released. More than four months after her death, her posthumous collection *Lioness: Hidden Treasures*, featuring original tracks and covers, was released. It shot to the top of the album charts. A portion of its sales goes to a charity set up by her father, the Amy Winehouse Foundation, which works to prevent the effects of drug and alcohol misuse on young people. A year after her death, Winehouse was still one of the top pop music acts, having sold 1.2 million albums.

Winehouse did not court fame but it enveloped her anyway. Her sensitivity led her to try to block out the pain with drink and drugs, but they made her agony worse, not better. The tragedy is that Winehouse had conquered her drug addiction but did not live long enough to conquer her alcoholism, despite the best efforts of those who cared for her. Her music and sense of style both touched and influenced a generation. Her many fans remember her talent and outspoken wit rather than her low points, and she remains an iconic figure.

Just six months after Winehouse was laid to rest, the world lost another talented singer whose life was plagued by addiction: Whitney Houston. At the height of her fame in the 1980s and 1990s, she was one of the world's best-selling artists. However, her descent into a drug-addled hell saw the hits dry up – and her millions swallowed up by ruthless dealers. It is thought the superstar blew a $100 million fortune feeding her habit. In 2012, at the age of 48, Houston drowned in a bathtub at the Beverly Hilton Hotel in Beverly Hills, California; her drug use contributed to her tragic death.

Born in Newark, New Jersey, in 1963, Houston was the third and youngest child in a talented family with strong musical connections. Her mother Cissy was a Grammy-winning gospel singer, singers Dionne and Dee Dee Warwick were her cousins, and singer Aretha Franklin an honorary aunt. Houston's father John was a former soldier and he went on to manage his daughter's career. From the age of five, Houston sang weekly at the New Hope Baptist Church in Newark. By the age of 11, she was performing as a soloist. At 15, the pretty teenager was modelling and singing back-up vocals – including on Chaka Khan's hit 'I'm Every Woman'. Houston's big break came when she was 19 and was spotted singing in a New York nightclub, leading to legendary record producer Clive Davis signing her to his Arista record label.

Houston released her debut album, *Whitney Houston*, in 1985. In America, seven consecutive number one singles followed. Houston became famous worldwide, garnering awards and critical plaudits. In 1987, her second album, *Whitney*, became the first studio album by a female artist to enter the Billboard Hot 100 at number one. However, Houston's stardom seemed to go to her head. In 1988, she amazed fans at her final British gig by announcing: "I've had seven consecutive number ones – I'm bigger than The Beatles!"

The remark was met with a stony silence. Houston proved even less of a hit later on with stars at a £100,000 end-of-tour bash at posh London restaurant Les Ambassadeurs, as she kept the celebrities, among them Elton John and Boy George, waiting for two hours. Before Houston ungraciously made her entrance, she shoved past well-wishers outside the restaurant, pushed past guests, then disappeared into a private room. It was 1am and guests were preparing to leave. Houston held court in an upstairs room, while a minder plucked selected guests from the throng for a private audience. Boy George stormed out after two minutes, complaining she was a bitch. "What a rude cow," he said. "I've met most of the royal family, including Princess Diana, and they are more important than fucking Whitney Houston. Yet royalty wouldn't treat people that way. She made me feel like a nothing. Who does she think she is?"

Yet Britain's diva was America's sweetheart. Her golden-girl status reached its apex when she sang 'The Star-Spangled Banner' at the Super

Bowl in 1991 during the first Gulf War, and millions watching were moved to tears. In 1992, Houston made her film debut in *The Bodyguard*. It was a massive success and gave the singer her signature song – her cover of Dolly Parton's 'I Will Always Love You' became the biggest-selling single by a female artist in music history.

Sadly, things were about to change for Houston. The same year, she married Bobby Brown. The couple's daughter, Bobbi Kristina, was born in March 1993. Bobbi Kristina was Houston's only child and Brown's fourth. An American rapper and a self-styled bad boy, Brown found success after escaping a life of petty crime. Before Brown, Houston had had long-term relationships with two other high-profile stars: National Football League player Randall Cunningham and actor Eddie Murphy. Both relationships had been conducted in a low-key manner, failing to make headlines. Houston and Brown's marriage proved different. Soon it became clear that the couple were partners in self-destruction, as they made the news for using drugs, for drink and domestic violence, and for Brown's violent brawls and court appearances. As Houston's health slipped away, she squandered her talent, her record sales declined and her happiness seemed to disappear. Signs that the marriage was rocky came when the couple separated in 1995. In September, Brown was no longer wearing a wedding ring and announced: "Whitney and I are getting a divorce."

A month later, Brown entered the Betty Ford Center in California in a bid to win back his wife. It emerged she had dumped him after he began drinking a bottle of brandy a day as well as taking cocaine. Brown had hit the depths just days after splitting with Houston and being witness to the death of his bodyguard and future brother-in-law, Steven Sealy, when he was killed in a drive-by shooting in Boston. Brown was with Sealy when the bullets ripped into Brown's Bentley, and he ducked for cover under the steering wheel. The couple reconciled but continued to make headlines. By the time they celebrated their fourth anniversary in 1996, Brown had been arrested six times in six years.

In January 2000, airport security guards found marijuana in Houston's luggage when she and her husband were at Hawaii Airport. The couple still boarded their San Francisco-bound plane, however, which took off before police got to the airport. The case was dropped but she was axed from performing at the Oscars. After this event, Houston looked thinner and her behaviour was erratic as she turned up late for events and cancelled shows. Rumours circulated about her drug use and Houston was forced to issue a denial that she was hitting the hardest, most poisonous drug of all: crack. She talked about her heavy drug use for the first time in 2002, admitting to using alcohol, marijuana, cocaine and prescription pills. However, she emphatically denied taking crack. During an interview with American TV host Diane Sawyer, Houston hit out: "First of all, let's get one thing straight. Crack is cheap. I make too much money to ever smoke crack. Let's get that straight. Okay? We don't do crack. We don't do that. Crack is whack."

However, Houston did admit taking cocaine laced with cannabis, saying: "We were lacing our marijuana with base [cocaine] ... We were buying kilos and ounces and ounces."

The singer added: "The biggest devil is me. I'm either my best friend or my worst enemy."

By then, Houston's reputation was tarnished. Some blamed her relationship with Brown. However, Houston was already doing drugs when she met Brown. In 2013, Houston's elder brother Michael admitted that he was responsible for introducing her to drugs, including crack cocaine, in the 1980s. Limo driver Al Bowman, who drove Houston for two decades, told the *Daily Mirror* that when he worked for Houston it was she, not Brown, who made the most demands over drugs, saying: "Nine times out of ten it was Whitney who wanted to buy more drugs."

Bowman first drove Whitney around, with her mentor Davis, at the height of her fame in the mid-1980s. He said: "She was just a sweet girl back then, happy to be out of New Jersey. I would pick her and Clive up for red carpet events and ferry them back and forth. Whitney was so nice."

But as the years rolled by and Bowman drove the superstar more he said her transformation was astonishing: "Things took a turn for the worse when she met Bobby Brown in the early 1990s. They started smoking crack in the back of the limo. One time it got a little crazy back there, they were smoking and all of a sudden the limo is on fire. I pulled over and got the fire extinguisher and put the fire out. It turns out they were free-basing crack, it was like a crack lab in the back of the limo. There were little bags, pipes and spoons all over the place, they were using a little butane torch and lit up a bunch of cocktail napkins and the whole place went up. Whitney and Bobby had no clue what was going on, they were wasted and just wanted to party it up."

Bowman says her drug habit was so bad that Houston would ask him to drive her into Los Angeles' dangerous ghetto areas to get her next fix:

"She'd ask me to take her to Compton, a rough area of LA, to get crack. It was like a bad rap video. It would be super late after Whitney had been partying all night and I'd pull up in the shadiest neighbourhood I'd ever seen. Whitney would wind down the window and the dealers were as star struck as anyone else, they thought she was doing a benefit concert or something – but all she wanted was crack."

Houston would hand over rolls of $50 bills and the dealer would give her bags of crack cocaine, cocaine and cannabis. In the end her powerful voice was ruined by the effects of smoking crack. Eventually, in 2003, Bowman decided to stop working for Houston after her antics and crazy demands became excessive. He said: "Driving Whitney was never A to B, there was always a diversion, there was always a problem. She'd get so angry about traffic and always wanted me to be first at the lights. She had turned into a monster, real arrogant. She was a diva who felt she had that sense of entitlement. I told her to find another driver."

The same year, Brown was charged with hitting his wife. Houston called the police and claimed he hit her face during a violent row at their home in Atlanta, Georgia. The pop diva was left with a cut lip and a bruised cheek. Brown was charged with battery when he eventually turned himself in. Houston said Brown used his "hands and fists" after "threatening to beat her ass". When Houston appeared in court with her gaunt face badly bruised all appeared forgiven as the couple kissed and cuddled while police processed the case. She later dropped the charges.

In 2004, Brown and Houston starred in the TV reality show, *Being Bobby Brown*. It was a harrowing portrait, revealing the extent of Houston's physical and mental deterioration. Nevertheless, she spent time in the studio and was expected to make a comeback. That seemed unlikely when a photograph appeared in press in January 2005 showing the once beautiful woman with a now ravaged face and wild hair. The photograph was taken when she was spotted walking to a garage near her home in Atlanta, Georgia, at 4am, dressed in her pyjamas and a fur coat. Her struggle with alcohol and drugs had clearly come at a terrible price. One motorist said: "She was like a bag lady in an expensive coat. She looked horrible."

Houston went into rehab, and filed for divorce in September 2006. When the singer appeared at a Beverly Hills charity gala the next month, she had returned to her glamorous best, looking both happy and healthy. In 2007, Houston appeared to have achieved her comeback. In April, she divorced from Brown, taking custody of their daughter. In October, she flew to London to make a sensational surprise appearance at the Royal Albert Hall for the Fashion Rocks show. There were gasps in the auditorium when the singer stepped on to the stage in a dazzling floor-length mermaid white Valentino gown to introduce the final catwalk show of the night. Not only did Houston sport a new, cleaner, leaner, healthier figure, she appeared to have abandoned her former diva ways. Gone were the outrageous demands, as she only wanted a glass of water for her voice before she made her grand entrance. She went on stage and sang only one incredible note – reassuring her fans "The Voice" was back. Her ever loyal producer, Davis, coaxed her back into the studio as she gained a $10 million record deal but the results were mediocre. Those hoping Houston would recover with Brown out of her life were to be disappointed: there were too many concerts cancelled and too many shambolic performances.

In September 2009, Houston gave her first interview in seven years, telling chat show host Oprah Winfrey about her drug abuse and her marriage to Brown: "He slapped me once, but he got hit on the head three times by me. At home, he was very much the father, he was very much the man. He was very much in control. I liked that. When he said something, I listened. I was very interested in having someone have that kind of control over me. It was refreshing."

Houston revealed that her drug use became "heavy" shortly after their wedding, adding that she would take marijuana combined with cocaine, and telling Winfrey: "You put your marijuana, you lace it, you roll it up and you smoke it."

The singer added: "He was my drug. I didn't do anything without him. I wasn't getting high by myself. It was me and him together. We were partners."

A month later, Houston appeared on *The X Factor* in Britain as a guest mentor. Her performance was widely slated and it seemed that her flawless voice was gone forever. She struggled through her UK tour in 2010. While her vocals often let her down, she gave her all. She was adored by her entourage and joked about bad reviews. Backstage, she was at her best, she was happy, saying: "I have never felt so good."

In May 2011, Houston enrolled in a rehab centre as an outpatient. It remains unclear which specific demons the singer was battling. Her representative said: "Whitney voluntarily entered the program to support her long-standing recovery process."

FALLEN IDOLS

Tragically, Houston's recovery proved an impossible task. On 11th February 2012, she was found dead in the bath at her suite at the Beverly Hilton Hotel in Beverly Hills. Detectives discovered powder and a spoon with white residue – found to be cocaine – in her hotel room. The star was at the hotel because she was due to appear at a pre-Grammy Awards event there, hosted by her mentor, Davis. Shortly before 2pm, she went to her suite on the fourth floor of the hotel. With the contents of her suitcases strewn across the king-size bed and her gown for the evening hanging in the wardrobe, she told aides at 2.40pm she was going for a soak in the bath. Houston later used a phone in the bathroom to call her mother Cissy at her New Jersey home at 3.15pm. Her entourage had taken over most of the hotel's fourth floor and her hairdresser, stylist and two bodyguards were waiting for the star in her suite. But at 3.42pm her concerned hairdresser went in to check on her – and let out a piercing scream. A bodyguard ran in to the bathroom and saw the singer's face was under the water. A family source said her legs were up out of the water – as though she had slid down the back of the bath. One bodyguard hauled the singer's body out of the bath while another alerted security. Staff called 911 and explained that the star was unconscious. Firefighters – already at the hotel helping to prepare for the party below – rushed up to the fourth floor and began CPR in a futile attempt to revive her. Sources described the scene as "horrific", with friends and relatives screaming. Minutes later, paramedics arrived and continued to perform CPR. But it was apparent no more could be done and Houston was declared dead at 3.55pm. Houston's daughter Bobbi Kristina and her cousin Dionne Warwick were allowed into the room, only to break down in tears.

Detectives followed standard procedure and asked everyone to leave the room, sealing it off as a crime scene. As the police searched the room, guests were arriving for the party downstairs. Los Angeles County Coroner officials and hotel bosses eventually agreed to take Houston's body out of a back exit to avoid the media scrum. Shortly before 2am, paramedics wheeled a stretcher out of the hotel and into a coroner's white Ford van.

Speculation mounted around the belief that Houston's death was drug related, and hotel guests said she had been seen acting erratically in the 48 hours leading up to her demise. Footage from a party on the eve of her death showed her looking the worse for wear and behaving strangely. In March, Los Angeles Coroner's officials revealed that Houston drowned in a hotel bath as a result of taking cocaine. The report said the singer's death was also due to a previously unreported heart disease that caused blockages in her arteries. Other drugs were found in her bloodstream – including marijuana, Xanax, the muscle relaxant Flexeril and the allergy medication Benadryl. But the Los Angeles Coroner's spokesman said cocaine was the only one that contributed to Houston's death and that toxicology tests showed she was a chronic cocaine user. Several bottles of prescription pills were found in her room, but coroner's officials said they were not in excessive quantities and no foul play was suspected. Her death was ruled as accidental. The final autopsy report issued a month later confirmed that Houston had cocaine in her bloodstream on the day she died. She also had a build-up of plaque in her arteries, which can restrict blood flow – the condition is common in drug users.

Even in death, Houston was the focus of a media frenzy when American magazine, the *National Enquirer*, splashed a photograph of Houston in her coffin over its front page. The harrowing image sparked fury among Houston's family and fans. The picture was taken at a funeral home in Newark, New Jersey. It showed the star wearing a blue dress and £400,000-worth of jewellery.

Many believed that, at the time of her death, Houston had been struggling to cope with the pressure of being back in the spotlight. She was due to release her film *Sparkle*, loosely based on the story of The Supremes, in the summer of 2012. The singer was big news again after years out of the unforgiving glare of the showbiz limelight. She was also upset and feeling "vulnerable" over criticism of her failed singing comeback, which saw her album *I Look to You* panned by critics. Perhaps the level of pressure on her frail emotional state led her to return to using drugs.

Houston fought addiction for many years and had spells in rehab in an effort to beat her problems. When she died, her voice was ravaged by years of drug use, but recordings at her peak remain her legacy, along with her influence on numerous female singers. Houston had phenomenal commercial success and, by the end of her life, achieved record sales close to 200 million. Her record-breaking 415 career awards included two Emmys and six Grammys. Such an achievement will be hard to beat, ensuring her place in music history.

The slow, painful downfall of Houston and of the stars who went before her make for tough reading. Did their success exacerbate their addictions? Did their fame fuel stress? Or did the high points of their glittering careers make the downsides worthwhile? They remain iconic figures yet all of them appear to have been vulnerable and unable to manage life in the spotlight, however much they wanted it.

CHAPTER FOUR:

A TASTE FOR EXCESS

On the stage, pop stars are dynamic and exciting. Male rock musicians become like gods, worshipped by fans. Many have lived out a decadent rock and roll lifestyle, enjoying the access to women, groupies, alcohol and drugs that goes with it. As they reap the financial rewards of success they can afford to indulge in self-destructive habits, from overspending to overeating, from drug addictions to boozing that can ruin their health, looks, talent and careers. Some become as famous for drug busts and glamorous girlfriends as their music. They may find themselves living in a celebrity bubble, surrounded by hangers-on who mismanage their money, or worse. The list of names of those who have lived the sex, drugs and rock and roll dream to find out it is a nightmare is long: for some it had fatal consequences – and among them are the biggest names in music.

One of the 20th century's greatest cultural idols fell victim to the dark side of fame. The undisputed "King of Rock and Roll", Elvis Presley, changed popular music with songs and films that took rock and roll mainstream. His smooth voice created chart-topping hits worldwide. Ruggedly handsome, with swivel hips and gyrating moves he became a sex symbol. However, on 16th August 1977, when the crowned head of rock and roll was found dead on his bathroom floor in his pyjamas at the age of 42, he was a horrendous mockery of the dazzling sexy figure he once was. A victim of junk food like jelly sandwiches, overuse of prescription drugs and a lack of friends, he died alone, adored by millions, known to but a few.

The last years of Presley's life were troubled: he never recovered from the breakdown of his marriage to Priscilla Wagner and their divorce in 1973, he ballooned in size and he became a bloated caricature of his former self. He became addicted to prescription drugs and continued a hectic schedule of performances. A report revealed Presley had 10 drugs in his system when he died. There were rumours that he died of anaphylactic shock brought on by codeine pills. In the first eight months of 1977, his main physician, Dr George C. Nichopoulos, prescribed him more than 10,000 doses of narcotics, sedatives and amphetamines. Nichopoulos was exonerated of criminal liability for the singer's death. In 1994, an investigation was reopened into Presley's death that concluded he died of a heart attack, although his use of multiple prescription drugs was a factor in his declining health.

Years of high living took their toll on his waistline, which swelled to 44 inches. They also hit his finances. When Presley died, he was on the verge of bankruptcy. The man who relied on others to take care of business was about to have his assets seized and be thrown out of his mansion home, Graceland, in Memphis, Tennessee. Rather than chartering flights on his concert tours, Presley bought his own Convair 880 airliner for more than $1 million, then spent another $750,000 kitting it out with two bathrooms featuring 24-carat gold sinks, and two huge bedrooms. According to one estimate, he bought 2,000 cars during his lifetime, most of which he gave away. On one holiday to Denver, he stopped at a car dealership and bought five vehicles for $100,000. On another occasion, he bought and gave away 14 Cadillacs in one day.

If Presley's addiction to prescription drugs and junk food were helping to kill him, his manager, Colonel Tom Parker, was also bleeding him dry. In 1965, Presley earned $5.2 million, yet after paying Parker and his management company, he came away with just $1 million. In the same year Parker said his client was the highest-paid entertainer in the world, earning $1 million per annum. He failed to mention that his own commission was $1.5 million – making him the best-paid manager in show business.

However, the Presley myth, the legend and the music, especially the music, live on. Graceland became a place of pilgrimage. A shopping mall, hotel and car museum, all with a Presley theme, sprung up around the house in the 1980s. By the end of the decade, 650,000 visitors were passing through Graceland's doors every year, second only in America to the White House. Elvis Presley Enterprises' licensing arm employs a global network of agents to promote his name. No image that portrays Presley as anything less than perfect is approved, hence the absence of T-shirts featuring the singer during his final years. He is an American cultural icon, and his tragic deterioration is mourned as an example of how fame can ruin lives.

The "King of Pop" Michael Jackson suffered a similarly tragic fate. He died on 25th June 2009, aged 50, from an overdose of the powerful anaesthetic Propofol. When Jackson died, his body had become so frail paramedics failed to recognize the superstar, believing he was a hospice patient returning home to die.

Jackson's story is of a boy who became the King of Pop in a momentous music career spanning more than 30 years. He began his rise to world superstardom at the age of five when his father Joseph formed The Jackson Five with Michael's elder brothers Jackie, Tito, Marlon and Jermaine. Michael's cheeky grin beneath a distinctive Afro haircut won the hearts of the American nation. The group's first-ever hit, 'Big Boy', was released in January 1967. Michael soon became the focal point of the group, winning over audiences with his massive voice and exciting dance moves, which became his trademark. The Jackson Five became the biggest Motown soul band of the 1970s. While in The Jackson Five, in 1972, Michael launched his solo career with his first single 'Got to be There'. His second album, Thriller, became the biggest selling LP of all time, helping him win eight Grammy awards. It also marked the birth of his Moonwalk dance.

When Jackson left the group, it became apparent that the shy entertainer was unhappy. In an interview in the early 1980s, he revealed that his father had abused him and his brothers as children. Jackson struggled to cope with the loneliness of being such a huge star and was reported to have said:

"Even at home I'm lonely. It's so hard to make friends. I sometimes walk around the neighbourhood, just hoping to find someone to talk to."

In 1988, he bought land in California for $17 million and built the Disneyland-style Neverland Ranch, with a fairground and zoo. In the mid-1990s, he married and divorced Elvis Presley's daughter Lisa Marie. In 1996, he married nurse Deborah Jeanne Rowe and they had a son, Michael Joseph Jackson Jr, known as Prince Michael Jackson I, and a daughter, Paris-Michael Katherine. The couple divorced in 1999. His third child, Prince Michael II, was born in 2002 to an unnamed surrogate mother. That same year, the media slammed Jackson for dangling the baby out of a hotel window while in Berlin.

Jackson died in 2009, shortly before his comeback "This Is It" concert series was due to start. The singer's career had suffered after an allegation of child abuse in the mid-1990s but the case was settled out of court and no formal charges were brought. In 2005, he was tried and acquitted of further child-abuse allegations. Jackson's early demise meant he never made the triumphant return to the glory days that his fans wished. An investigation into his death revealed that Jackson's personal physician, Dr Conrad Murray, was responsible for administering the fatal anaesthetic – he got four years jail for involuntary manslaughter. In 2013, Jackson's mother Katherine, together with his three children, sued "This Is It" concert promoter AEG Live for £31 billion. The family accused "ruthless" bosses at the company of being so greedy they ended up killing him by ignoring his frail health. Jackson was never able to shake off allegations of child abuse, although he vehemently protested his innocence. The allegations meant he became a controversial figure. Nevertheless, he was undisputedly one of the greatest ever entertainers and is recognized as the most successful entertainer of all time by *Guinness World Records*.

Years before either Presley or Jackson met their deaths, "Britain's Bing Crosby", singer Michael Holliday, died in hospital at the age of 34 after an overdose of Nembutal sleeping pills on 29th October 1963. Ruggedly handsome, with greased-back hair, he was a heart-throb, chart-topping singer and TV star with his own show: *Mike on Holliday*. In the late 1950s, he had a string of hit singles, including his most famous number one, 1958's 'The Story of my Life'. Few people knew the real, sad story. On TV and the stage, sporting casual sweaters and laid back in a rocking chair he appeared relaxed and confident. Behind the scenes, he was a worrier and suffered from stage fright.

Holliday was born Norman Milne in Liverpool in 1928. He went to sea as a cabin boy in the Merchant Navy and entered show business after winning a talent contest imitating popular American crooner Bing Crosby. Holliday continued to imitate Crosby, and in 1951 went to work as an entertainer at a Butlin's holiday camp. Two years later, he joined radio regulars the Eric Winstone Band. An ambitious man, Holliday wrote to the BBC in 1954 asking for a TV audition. He got one and made his TV debut. A talent scout for EMI's Columbia saw Holliday on TV and signed him to the record label in 1955.

When the 1960s arrived, they did not bode well for Holliday. Teenagers were not interested in the music that their parents liked. His style of ballad was falling out of fashion and he was unable to change with the times. His last record, 'Little Boy Lost', reached number 50 in the charts in September 1960 for a week. With record sales falling and mounting debts, he had a nervous breakdown in September 1961. His wife, Margie, told the press: "[His] doctors say he must relax. I doubt if he will return to work until the end of the year." However, Holliday's behaviour eventually proved too much for his wife and the couple separated.

At 2am on 28th October 1963, Holliday gave what was his last performance at a nightclub on London's Charing Cross Road owned by his friend, 1948's world light-heavyweight boxing champion, Freddie Mills. Holliday sang 'I Can't Believe that You're in Love with Me'. The audience applauded as always. Mills said: "Mike was talking strangely. He told me: 'I'm giving it all up.' I told him I was sorry he had missed the cabaret and said he should come back the next night and see the show. He told me: 'I won't be coming back. Tonight is my last night.' I told him not to do anything stupid or ridiculous. He had a few drinks at the bar. I heard him say 'I want to get drunk quickly tonight.' My wife and he sat down at a table and she had a long talk with him to try to cheer him up. I gather he was talking about being parted from his wife."

Holliday left at 3.30am with a friend who was staying with the star at his house in Addington, Surrey. Later, the friend found Holliday slumped unconscious at the foot of the stairs. At 5am, Holliday was in hospital, where doctors fought in vain all day to save his life. It is unknown whether Holliday intended to take his own life. He made his last recording for Columbia the week before his death. In 1964, the record company released a tribute compilation EP *Memories of Mike*, which included a eulogy recorded by Holliday's idol Bing Crosby, whom he met in 1959. Holliday is remembered as one of Liverpool's first star musicians before The Beatles took the crown.

When Holliday died, the heady sex, drugs and rock and roll days of the Swinging Sixties were just about to start. The decade's most famous casualty is Brian Jones, the original leader of British band, the Rolling Stones. His drink- and drug-filled body was found in the swimming pool of his Sussex mansion in July 1969. He was just 27 years old. Within two years, rock stars Jimi Hendrix, Janis Joplin and Jim Morrison had all died from drug-related issues – all of them were aged only 27 at their deaths. The coincidence in ages led to what has been called the "27 Club", in a macabre reference to the early demise of some of the most talented musicians of modern times.

Pop guitarist Jones was a founding member, in 1962, of the Rolling Stones. He was also the group's most controversial member. Jones was twice convicted on drug charges and, during his court appearances, it was stated that he had been under psychiatric treatment for "pressures and tension". Jones was born in the genteel spa town of Cheltenham in Gloucestershire in 1942. He went on to become a brilliant pupil at Cheltenham Grammar School for Boys. A non-conformist from an early age, Jones was once suspended for leading a revolt against prefects, and admonished for campaigning against the school practice of wearing straw boaters in the summer and mortar boards in the winter. His parents influenced his interest in music: his mother was a piano teacher, and his father an aeronautical engineer and choirmaster at a local church.

Jones hated discipline of any kind and, when he left school, he did not relish the prospect of a nine-to-five job. Instead, he sought adventure in Europe, hitchhiking around and playing his harmonica in little bistros for a meal ticket.

When he returned home, Jones took a job as a coal-lorry driver but soon quit to find his way to London, where he met Mick Jagger and Keith Richards in a Soho pub. The year was 1961 and a revolution was dawning. The Rolling Stones were to become as much a part of it as The Beatles. Of all the five faces that became the Stones, two stood out: Jones with his blond hair cropped like a wig was idolized as much as Jagger. They were the two rebels and Keith Richards, Charlie Watts and Bill Wyman could not match them in the eyes of the fans.

Throughout Jones' career, he was cast in the eternal role of the rebel – the wild man in a wild business. But, in his own language, this wasn't his scene. Jones was an intense introvert – far removed from the rebel the fans knew. Neither did he glorify in the hysteria and uninhibited life of a Rolling Stone, once saying: "No one would choose to live the kind of life I lead. Do you really think I enjoy it? But I mustn't complain or be bitter about it. It's brought the bread and the opportunity."

With the band's success came the inevitable heartaches and hang-ups of the game. First were the girls, most famously Jones' relationship with model Anita Pallenberg, who left him for fellow band member Richards after Jones behaved violently towards her. Jones' love for the ladies began years before he became a star. Five different women bore him illegitimate children – some when they were just teenagers – although in one instance Jones did not know that he had fathered a child. Jones never went to see his children or sent them gifts or cards. His later romances made headlines. There were rumours of marriage, but the Rolling Stone would laugh at the prospect: "That's not my scene, man."

Why were there so many women in Jones' life? Perhaps the best answer came from the lips of the mother of his second child, Pat Andrews, when she told the press after he died: "He had to have girls around him because of his insecurity. He had to prove his male instincts. The funny thing is, I think that we all still love him in one way or another. He was the hardest boy in the world to understand and I think we all believed we could understand him if we tried long enough … But really no one ever could."

Another cause of heartache was Jones' discontentment with his role in the Rolling Stones as he lost creative control. Jones was often sore that practically all the group's records were composed by Jagger and Richards, and his compositions were ignored, saying: "It's not that I dislike their music. It's great. But there must be a fair crack at the whip. As a group we've got to consider all channels of music, mine included."

The pressures of fame, and Jones' feeling of being overshadowed by Jagger and Richards, often led him to the verge of nervous breakdown and deep depression. The most toxic part of the recipe that led to Jones' downfall was his drug use. In May 1967, two month after Pallenberg ended their relationship, he was arrested for possessing drugs. Drugs squad detectives who searched his flat in South Kensington found 11 objects that either contained or bore traces of drugs. A total of 35¼ grains of cannabis, which would make between seven and 10 cigarettes, were found. There was also a phial, which appeared to contain traces of cocaine. When the detectives asked Jones if the various articles belonged to him, and whether the substance was cannabis, he replied: "Yes, it is hash. I do smoke it. But not cocaine, man, that is not my scene."

When his case came to court in October, Jones admitted charges of possessing cannabis and allowing his flat to be used for the smoking of the drug. The prosecution accepted his plea of not guilty to a further charge of possessing cocaine and methedrine. Jones said he had taken drugs in the past to a slight extent, saying they had only brought him trouble and disrupted his career, and he hoped that would be an example to others. However, the judge told Jones that allowing premises to be used for the purpose of smoking cannabis was a very serious offence: "It means that people can break the law in comparative privacy and avoid detection of what is a growing canker in this country at the moment. Although no blame attaches to you for that phial of cocaine, it shows what happens at that sort of party. People who go there are smokers of cannabis. Others take hard drugs and that is how the rot starts."

Perhaps because of his fame and to set an example, Jones was sentenced to nine months in jail and ordered to pay costs. However, the prison sentence was squashed at appeal two months later, when psychiatrists and lawyers painted a picture of a vulnerable, sensitive and unstable young man with a tormented mind. Three psychiatrists told the court of Jones' psychological state, describing him as an "extremely frightened young man", who was very immature, emotionally unstable and possibly suicidal. Jones' counsel described his client's agony since the sentence was pronounced, saying that the musician's suffering had meant "more for him than perhaps it would ninety-nine out of 100 people". His lawyer added: "It may sound trite but Jones has suffered every single day since sentence was passed upon him – a suffering which cannot be removed and may be regarded as penalty enough."

Jones, he said, was a highly intelligent and extremely sensitive young man who had been catapulted to fame. This had not so much gone to his head as imposed an additional strain upon an "already fragile mental make-up". Psychiatrist Dr Anthony Flood stated that Jones had spent three weeks during the summer under his care: "My concern since his last appearance in court has been trying to calm his apprehensions as well as treat his underlying illness ... I think if one put a reefer within half a mile of Brian Jones he would start running."

Another psychiatrist, Lindesay Neustatter, told the judges about four interviews which he had with Jones: "He came in the most extraordinary clothes which one could only describe as flamboyant. I think he had gold trousers and something which looked like a fur rug." Surprisingly, Neustatter added, he found the man inside the clothes to be quiet, thoughtful and courteous. The court evidently took the doctors' opinions on board and set aside Jones' prison sentence. Jones was placed on probation for three years on the charge of possessing cannabis and fined the maximum amount possible, £1,000, although the judge conceded: "A fine is designed to hit the pocket, but no permitted fine could really hit this young man's pocket."

Despite such a close escape, Jones was back in the dock the next year. In May 1968, he was arrested a second time for possession of cannabis.

Police raided his flat in Chelsea and found 144 grains of cannabis in a ball of blue wool on a bureau on top of a Rolling Stones record. Jones claimed it had been left there by a previous tenant. When police interviewed the former tenant in America, she said she believed the wool was probably hers but denied any knowledge of the drug. When the case came to trial in September, Jones took to the witness box and said he had not used cannabis since his conviction the previous year: "Last year's conviction made me very frightened of the drug. To take it now would make me very nervous indeed."

He told the jury that the earlier drugs charges had affected the Rolling Stones and his career: "The trouble had set the group back. When this raid came we had been working on a new LP and a new single. We all felt that this new LP was going to lead us back to success."

Jones said that because of his emotional state when they found the cannabis he might have told the police that the ball of wool was his: "I might have said anything but I don't knit. I don't darn socks. I don't have a girlfriend who darns socks."

When the jury found him guilty of possessing drugs, Jones buried his head in his hands and rocked unsteadily on his feet: the star was sure he was going to jail because he was in breach of his probation order. Two prison officers guarding him in the dock had to help him to his seat. In the public gallery, several girls began crying. Jones' career looked to be stone dead. However, when the judge announced his decision Jones was able to smile with relief: he was fined £50. The judge said: "At the moment you are on probation from this court and you really must watch your step."

Jones was not proud of the drugs trials he faced and came through. Nevertheless, they haunted what was left of his short career. His second arrest presented problems when it came to him getting a visa to go on tour with the Rolling Stones to America. On top of this, his substance abuse, legal problems and state of mind had meant he had become increasingly difficult to work with. His input to the band was erratic. In a sudden announcement, Jones quit the Rolling Stones in June 1969. He said: "The Stones' music is not to my taste any more, I want to play my own kind of music. We had a friendly meeting and agreed that an amicable termination was the only answer."

The group's leader, Jagger, said: "Brian wants to play music which is more his own rather than always playing ours. We have decided he is best to be free to follow his own inclinations. But we part on the best of terms. We will continue to be friends. Obviously you cannot break up a friendship after so long."

Jones said he would devote his future to a new musical unit he was about to form. What fans did not know was that Jones had been kicked out of the Rolling Stones over his drug problems. Jones attempted to avoid the spotlight and spent time at his new home, which he had bought eight months earlier: Cotchford Farm, a 15th-century farmhouse in Hartfield, Sussex. The house was where A A Milne had written his immortal *Winnie the Pooh* stories, and Jones told his friends: "I'm the new Pooh of Pooh Corner."

Jones gave one or two small parties for close friends at the farmhouse but he mainly kept to himself, working on his own musical project. Just three weeks after his parting with the Rolling Stones, on 3rd July, friends found the 27-year-old Jones dead at his home. Friends who had called at the house discovered his body in the swimming pool, and it appeared that he had died while taking a midnight swim.

The Rolling Stones' tour manager, Tom Keylock, told the *Daily Mirror*: "I got a call from Brian's house, and the voice said there was trouble at the house. But when I rang Brian back there was no reply, and I am extremely worried."

When told the news of Jones' death, Keylock said: "This is a terrible shock. I spoke to Brian yesterday morning and he was full of spirits and raring to go."

The day after Jones' death, the press announced that the latest woman in his life, 22-year-old Swedish student Anna Wohlin, had gone into hiding – less than 24 hours after she had vainly tried to save him from death. Wohlin had been his companion for three months. She had been swimming with Jones in the pool at his home. For a few minutes, she went inside the house. When she returned, Jones was lying unconscious in the water. Desperately, she tried to give him the kiss of life, but Jones was dead.

Two other women in Jones' life said they would try to claim a share of his fortune – for two illegitimate sons he fathered. The day Jones died, Pat Andrews told the *Daily Mirror*: "I have got to think of the future of our son Mark, who is now seven. All we have received is 50 shillings a week from Brian under the court order and we are having to live in a London hostel because we have no other money."

Another claim on Jones' estate was pressed by Linda Lawrence, the mother of Jones' fourth child, Julian, then aged five. Her father, a builder from Windsor, said: "Brian made a settlement of £1,000. But this only paid for some bills he left behind."

Meantime, the Rolling Stones had cut their first single without Jones, 'Honky Tonk Women'. It was released the day after Jones' death and went on to top the charts in Britain and America. The group was also scheduled to perform a free concert in Hyde Park on 5th July, just two days after Jones' death. The group decided to dedicate their performance to their former band member.

When Jones' death was announced, it was believed that he died after an attack of asthma, from which he had suffered since childhood. A pathologist report showed there were traces of sleeping tablets, pep pills and alcohol in his bloodstream. The coroner ruled Jones died from "drowning by immersion in fresh water associated with severe liver dysfunction caused by fatty degeneration and ingestion of alcohol and drugs". The inquest recorded a verdict of death by misadventure.

However, even in death, Jones did not find peace and there have been a string of conspiracy theories surrounding his death. In 1994, two books were published that named a disgruntled East End builder hired to renovate Jones' house, Frank Thorogood, as Jones' murderer. Published after Thorogood's death so he could no longer sue for libel, Geoffrey Giuliano's *Paint it Black: The Murder of Brian Jones* and Terry Rawlings' *Brian Jones: Who Killed Christopher Robin?* alleged that the one-eyed Thorogood held Jones' head under the water until he drowned. Thorogood always maintained to police that he dived in to save Jones but arrived too late. The police were very interested in Giuliano's claim that he was contacted by a mystery East End thug who confessed to him on tape: "I want it off my shoulders – it's getting me down."

The mystery man described how a man known as "Frank" had started dunking Jones beneath the water in "horseplay". When Jones pleaded to be released his cries were ignored. "When he died it was easy. We didn't even know he was dead," said the thug.

However, the police did not reopen the case. Jones' last girlfriend, Wohlin, who also insisted he was murdered, in 2001 published her account of the events surrounding his death. Director Stephen Woolley bought the film rights to her, Giuliano's and Rawlings' books, and in 2005 released his film *Stoned*, which is a fictional account of Jones' life and death. In 2006, fan Trevor Hobley claimed he could prove the guitarist was murdered. Hobley spent three years investigating Jones' death and said he had uncovered evidence that the star was killed. Hobley handed what he said was new evidence over to the Attorney General and called for the star's body to be exhumed so it could be examined using modern methods.

Matters reached fever pitch in 2009, when investigative journalist Scott Jones – no relation to the guitarist – handed the police new evidence, suggesting that Thorogood killed Brian Jones in a fight and that police at the time had been involved in a cover-up. Scott claimed that Brian received death threats before he died. Scott interviewed the nurse who found Brian's body in the pool, Janet Lawson, who said Brian had been unhappy with Thorogood's renovation work and had sacked the builder that day. Lawson told Scott: "There was something in the air. Frank was acting strangely, throwing his weight around a bit."

She described how Brian had asked for his asthma inhaler and, when she was in the house looking for it, Thorogood came in: "Frank came in in a lather. His hands were shaking. He was in a terrible state. I thought the worst almost straight away and went to the pool to check. When I saw Brian on the bottom of the pool and was calling for help, Frank initially did nothing. I shouted for Frank again as I ran towards the house, and he burst out before I reached it, ran to the pool and instantly dived in. But I had not said where Brian was. I thought, 'How did he know Brian was at the bottom of the pool?'"

At the time Lawson did not tell the police about the tension between Thorogood and Brian, nor of her suspicions. She believed that Thorogood killed the star in an incident of horseplay gone wrong, telling Scott: "I went into the house to look for Brian's inhaler. Frank jumped back in the pool, did something to Brian and by the time I came back, Brian was lying peacefully on the bottom of the pool with not a ripple in the water. I think because of the state that Frank was in, something had to have happened. I mean, why would Frank have been standing in the kitchen absolutely terrified if something hadn't happened?"

Scott revealed that the first police officer on the scene, PC Albert Evans, suspected Thorogood had killed Brian in a fight. The policeman had no evidence to support his feelings and was not asked to attend the inquest into Brian's death. Scott also claimed that although the Rolling Stones' tour manager Tom Keylock said he was not at Brian's house the night he died, he was actually inside the house with Lawson when the fight started. Scott suggested that Keylock had installed Lawson, who was his girlfriend, at Brian's house because he sensed the star was unwell and in some danger, then, after his death, cleared the house of evidence and pressured witnesses not to talk to the police about Thorogood.

The Sussex Police reviewed Scott's evidence, including 600 pages of new testimonies from people who were at the star's house the night he died. In 2010, the police concluded that there was no new evidence to suggest that the coroner's original verdict of "death by misadventure" was incorrect and said that they would not reopen the investigation.

The continuing popularity of the Rolling Stones in the 21st century means that fans have not forgotten Brian Jones, even if some of them may not have been born when he was alive. He was a strong swimmer but he suffered from asthma: when he died he had been drinking heavily and had taken pills. Speculation regarding the circumstances surrounding his death will no doubt continue as long as the band he founded is successful, casting him as fame's ultimate victim, killed by a man jealous of his stardom and all the perks it brought.

British punk rock band the Sex Pistols became a public enemy in the summer of 1977 with their number one single, the anti-royalist 'God Save the Queen', released during Queen Elizabeth II's Silver Jubilee. A TV interview for the *Today* show in which Bill Grundy provoked the band into swearing raised the group's profile even more. The Sex Pistols' manager, art school dropout Malcolm McLaren, orchestrated a private party on a boat on the River Thames on which they performed in front of the Houses of Parliament. The party – as was so often the case with any Sex Pistols activity – degenerated into complete chaos. Police raided it and arrested the group.

Punk was associated with mischief, outrageous humour and bags of attitude, as it tweaked the Establishment's nose until it squealed. The Sex Pistols' music was not played on radio, concert venues banned them, shops refused to sell their records and the band passed through the hands of various record companies who dropped the group when they found them too hot to handle. Nevertheless, record sales soared. Fans felt like rebels, revolutionaries and anarchists as they adopted spiky hair, safety pins, razor blades and pogo dancing. The band's popularity was short-lived: they split the following year and, by 1979, their bass guitarist and gangly poster boy, Sid Vicious, was dead at the age of 21.

The Sex Pistols formed in London in 1975. The line-up included lead singer John Lydon, aka Johnny Rotten, guitarist Steve Jones, drummer Paul Cook and bassist Glen Matlock. When Matlock left the band in February 1977, Vicious was recruited as his replacement. Born John Simon Ritchie in Lewisham in 1957, Vicious' parents separated when he was a child. Later his mother, Anne, married and assumed her husband's surname, Beverley. She was widowed six months later. Vicious was a friend of Lydon's, who named him "Sid" after a pet hamster. The "Vicious" suffix happened because the hamster tried to bite him.

Vicious was one of the Sex Pistols' biggest fans, even inventing the pogo dance of jumping up and down while watching the band as a way of bumping into fans he did not like. Although Vicious' guitar-playing skills were then only nascent, his look and wild attitude made him ripe to become the iconic face of punk rock. At concerts, Vicious stabbed himself with knives and broken glass. He swore, belched and vomited on stage, and spat at his audiences. Vicious told the *Daily Mirror* what had turned him into a punk rocker: school. The teachers, he said, "taught me nothing". Vicious would admit to only one weakness: he loved his mother, telling the newspaper: "I'm not a vicious person really. I consider myself kind-hearted. I love my mum." His mother said of him: "His public image isn't justified. He's only violent on the surface."

However, Vicious' career with the Sex Pistols was overshadowed by his relationship with American blonde erotic dancer Nancy Spungen, who the press soon labelled "Nauseating Nancy" for her violent behaviour and verbal abuse. A notorious groupie and heroin addict with mental health issues, Spungen had travelled to London with the aim of getting involved with the Sex Pistols. After Lydon rejected her, she and Vicious struck up a passionate yet toxic partnership that was to prove their downfall. Spungen introduced Vicious to heroin and he contracted hepatitis – a liver complaint – from using dirty needles. As the pair led the destructive life of junkies, so Vicious became alienated from his fellow band members. He confessed to being on a path of self-destruction.

While on tour in Holland in December 1977, Vicious told the *Daily Mirror*: "I want to self-destruct myself. Look at my arms. That's a bottle scar from when I cut myself. Look at my chest." He showed off his left arm, which had a nine-inch scar halfway up it, and his scarred chest: "I'm going to commit suicide." Lydon responded: "Oh. No. You are not. We're the stars round here not you. You'd become more famous than me and I'd get jealous. You're just a cheap imitation bass player. You're sick. We're going to put you in a clinic. You are addicted to trash."

Vicious seemed to have an addiction to broken glass. He smashed a bottle in the tour bus and dropped a glass on the floor. The conversation turned to Vicious' sex life: "I'm not very interested in straight sex. I like perversions. I like buying gear to strap myself down."

Curiously, the staff at the hotel where the Sex Pistols were staying took a liking to the band. Late at night, when Vicious ordered his fourth ice cream, the kitchen staff made one three-foot high. While every member of the band expressed horror at Vicious' uncouth behaviour, they were always to be found looking after him and trying to stop him landing in trouble. The newspaper reporter noted the Sex Pistols had three saving graces: talent, vast energy and enormous wit. They knew their greatest liability was Vicious and did their best to look after him. However, there was tension within the band because of his relationship with Spungen: they blamed her for his behaviour and tried to separate them.

The same month, on the eve of a million-dollar money-spinning tour, the Sex Pistols were banned from America. The official reason for the ban, which came from the American embassy in London, was: "moral turpitude". Behind that phrase of official American disapproval was the fact that all four band members had criminal records. Manager McLaren said angrily: "It's true the lads have records for cat burglary, assault and suchlike, but they were juveniles at the time."

He vowed the band would not stay quiet about the ban and would fight it. Somehow, they managed to get visas. The Sex Pistols set off on what was an eventful tour, getting star treatment with massive publicity on local TV stations, newspapers and magazines. Vicious was suffering symptoms of heroin withdrawal and – desperate to get a fix – his behaviour became increasingly odd. There was a showdown in San Antonio, Texas, when the group played their third concert: sheriff's deputies ended up storming the stage after a battle between the Sex Pistols and fans in which Vicious battered a man over the head with his guitar. The fracas began after the group started to yell insults at the 2,000 fans, with Lydon telling them: "So this is Texas manhood. You're all a load of faggots." The crowd retaliated by pelting the Sex Pistols with beer cans, pies and lighted cigarettes. A pie was shoved in Vicious' face, and he was hit in the mouth with a beer can. Then one fan tried to climb on to the stage. Vicious brought his guitar down on the fan's head three times before a sheriff's deputy slapped handcuffs on the fan and led him away. The guitarist – who gashed his arm "for fun" with a broken bottle earlier in the tour – said later: "My guitar strap keeps breaking, don't it?"

When the band played Dallas, Texas, Vicious was given a bloody nose by a girl fan. He smeared the blood all over his face and bare chest as the audience screamed with delight. Vicious shouted at security men to keep back as the girl connected with a swinging punch. He yelled to the men: "Get off, get off. This is great!"

Later that month, Vicious managed to get some heroin and, overdosing, fell unconscious. Manager McLaren got to him just in time to save him. The band was falling apart and Vicious' addiction was taking its toll on them all. After arriving in New York at the end of the tour, Lydon revealed that the group had decided to split up. He told newsmen: "I'm sick of working with the Sex Pistols. I never want to appear with them again."

Only hours afterwards, Vicious was carried unconscious off a plane after swallowing a knockout mixture of drink and drugs. The bass guitarist was flying from Los Angeles to New York when he passed out. The pilot alerted New York's Kennedy Airport that he had a sick man on board. A waiting ambulance rushed Vicious to the nearby Jamaica Hospital, where he was put on a drip machine and heart monitor as doctors gave him oxygen and a drugs antidote. Vicious discharged himself from the hospital two days later. Road manager John Tiberi, who travelled with Vicious, said he had not fully recovered from the effects of hepatitis: "Sid had downed a lot of scotch, perhaps a bottle. And then he took two or three Valium pills because he is nervous of flying."

In London, a spokesman for Virgin Records confirmed that the Sex Pistols were parting company. He said that Jones and Cook had flown to Brazil for a holiday with their "hero", British fugitive and jailbreaker Ronald Biggs, who was wanted for his part in the Great Train Robbery of 1963. Although the Sex Pistols were minus Lydon and Vicious, Jones and Cook continued on without them, releasing a single called 'No One is Innocent', which maintained their record as the sickest punk band of the time. Biggs replaced Lydon on vocals. Among the lyrics were the tasteless lines: "God save Martin Bormann / And Nazis on the run ... / God save Myra Hindley / God save Ian Brady." The BBC refused to play the song but that did not stop it climbing the charts. Jones and Cook also revealed that the band was making a film featuring Biggs, *The Great Rock 'n' Roll Swindle*, which was released in 1980. A fictionalized satire about the band's rise and split, the film shows Vicious tottering down a staircase singing his own raw, raucous version of the song 'My Way', popularized by Frank Sinatra. When Vicious has finished singing, he takes out a pistol and starts shooting at the audience. Vicious was so ill that he had to record the song one line at a time.

Vicious struck out on a solo career with Spungen as his manager. Before that could get off the ground, she was dead and he was charged with her murder. Spungen was discovered dead in the Room 100 apartment she shared with Vicious at the Chelsea Hotel in Manhattan, New York, on 12th October. Wearing only a black bra and panties, Spungen's body was found lying in a pool of blood in the bathroom. She had been beaten and stabbed in the stomach. Vicious came out of a drug coma and found her dead. He raised the alarm by dialling room service, saying "there is something wrong". Then he rushed downstairs shouting: "Something has happened to my girl." Horrified hotel staff found Spungen's body and Vicious was arrested. As he was led from the hotel, he shouted to the crowd that had gathered: "Why don't you sod off?" A porter told the press: "He was in a very upset condition and kept saying: 'She's dead, she's dead.'"

Vicious was taken to a drug treatment centre and then transferred to the notoriously tough prison, Rikers Island. Police sergeant Thomas Kilroy told reporters: "He admitted he killed her during a dispute." The policeman said that drug implements, but no drugs, were found in the couple's apartment. He claimed that when Vicious was arrested his "impression was that he was high". Friends of the punk rocker said that Vicious had been taking "a really high dose" of methadone, which is used to wean addicts off heroin. Vivienne Westwood, the girlfriend of the Sex Pistols' manager, McLaren, said: "Sid does have a temper, but he loves Nancy very much. He and Nancy did have a drugs problem, but Sid was taking a cure course to come off heroin." Only six weeks earlier Spungen had told her parents: "I'll never make it to twenty-one. I'll go out in a blaze of glory."

Other people had had a premonition that the couple's love was ill-fated. McLaren admitted that he had been so determined to break up the romance that he and friends had tried to "kidnap" Spungen in London: "We had a one-way ticket to New York for her but she screamed blue murder in the middle of a street and we had to let her go." McLaren added: "Nancy was a bad influence on him. He certainly wasn't a heroin addict when he met her." In a bid to help the star, McLaren hired private detectives, saying: "Sid is not clear what happened. He was shocked when he found Nancy's body. It could be that she committed suicide or was murdered by someone else. We just don't know."

While Vicious waited to appear in court for a preliminary hearing, McLaren and Vicious' friends attempted to raise the bail required for his release. Vicious' lawyer said his client would plead not guilty. Vicious was quoted as saying he was asleep in his room when his girlfriend was stabbed. One friend who visited Vicious in jail said the punk rocker believed Spungen had either committed suicide, or was killed by an intruder.

The press reported that the bizarre and chilling games played by Vicious began with a gift from Spungen: a razor-sharp flick knife. According to friends, it became his obsession. He would pick his teeth with the knife and sometimes even pretend to slit Spungen's throat with it. A friend of the couple, Pierre Benain, said: "I often saw Sid and Nancy playing the most sadistic and dangerous games just like a couple of kids. Sid was always fiddling with the knife Nancy gave him. He seemed obsessed with it. But even when he pretended to cut her throat it was only for fun. I can't believe he killed her. He was so madly in love with her he would never deliberately have harmed her. The trouble with Sid is that he gets terribly bored when he isn't appearing with his group, so he used to drink and take drugs and play those stupid games. Nancy was a junkie, so was he, so there was no way he could get away from drugs. I don't think Nancy was very good for him. Sid has done some silly things but basically he is just a lost kid. Not a murderer."

Vicious was released on bail after spending four days in the tough New York jail. For most of the time he was in a drugs unit being weaned off methadone. Vicious faced a jail sentence of 15 years or more if he was convicted. He told friends: "Now I'm going to prove my innocence."

Just days later, on 23rd October, Vicious was in hospital after slashing his wrists with a broken light bulb and a razor blade. He was said to have screamed at police: "I want to die. I want to join Nancy. I didn't keep my part of the bargain."

The gory suicide bid happened in a New York hotel where Vicious was staying. A police patrolman said: "When we went into the room he was struggling with a man who said he was Vicious' psychiatrist. The psychiatrist said that Vicious tried to jump out of the window on the eighth floor – but he restrained him."

Vicious, dressed only in his underpants, was taken by ambulance to a Manhattan hospital. Doctors put dozens of stitches into slashes in his wrists and forearms, and he was held in a psychiatric hospital. A judge ordered a psychological examination and a round-the-clock suicide watch on the star. British music writer Joe Stevens, who saw Vicious immediately after the suicide attempt, said: "He missed the main veins. He asked us for drugs – he said he wanted to join Nancy. He's starting to believe that he's going to have to spend twenty years in prison."

When Vicious left the hospital, he was allowed to keep his freedom on bail, provided he continued treatment for drug addiction. By November, he had found a new girlfriend, 22-year-old New York dress designer Michelle Robinson, who he met at a punk rock concert. In early December, Vicious was rearrested for assaulting the brother of American singer Patti Smith, Todd, with a bottle during a fight in a New York disco. Vicious served another 55 days in prison.

Vicious was granted bail of $50,000 but remained in prison on Rikers Island for two weeks because of a delay in the cash being transferred from Britain. On 1st February 1979, Vicious attended a hearing at a Manhattan court. Vicious appeared pale and drawn during the 10-minute hearing, during which his lawyer claimed he acted in self-defence, saying that a blood test ordered by the court would confirm that Vicious "had been assaulted and had suffered some injuries in that hotel room". The court ruled that he could be released on bail of $50,000. The date for his trial was due to be set on 1st March. Vicious' mother was at the hearing, watching from the public gallery. Later, as she waited for her son outside the court, she said: "The first thing I'm going to do is get him something to eat. He wants an enormous ice cream."

FALLEN IDOLS

Less than 24 hours later, Vicious was dead from an overdose of heroin. He was found naked in the arms of his new girlfriend, Robinson, at her seedy flat in New York's fashionable Greenwich Village. After walking from the courtroom, the couple went off to celebrate his freedom at a party in her flat. Vicious had been in a compulsory detoxification methadone programme for seven weeks while he was in jail at Rikers Island. He was clean from heroin.

Vicious' mother – herself once a registered addict – ordered some heroin for the party. Vicious injected himself with heroin at around midnight and collapsed shortly afterwards. His lips turned blue and he had a seizure for about 45 minutes. Vicious was revived and went to bed with his girlfriend Robinson at about 3am. The next morning, his mother took the couple a cup of tea in bed and frantically tried to wake Vicious, who had to report to the police as a condition of his bail. Anne told police she kissed him on the forehead to waken him but found he was cold and had no pulse. His girlfriend was completely unaware that he had died while they slept.

The first police officer on the scene that morning discovered a syringe, a spoon and possible heroin residue near the body. Police said they believed he had taken the overdose by accident. Anne claimed her son always took large amounts of heroin and although his last dose taken at the party was very strong, it was "no more than he was used to". Vicious' girlfriend, Robinson, claimed that he once threatened her with a knife. She told police: "We were having a row when he rushed into the kitchen and pulled out a knife as if he was going to stab me. Suddenly he dropped the knife and apologised."

Robinson also told murder detectives that Vicious was in the best of spirits and took a shot of heroin. She said he was walking around bouncing off walls and was really high "then he suddenly went purple and passed out". An autopsy confirmed Vicious died from an accumulation of fluid on the lungs, a characteristic of heroin abuse.

Anne revealed that her son's last wish was to be buried next to Spungen in Philadelphia's Jewish cemetery. Vicious was not Jewish, so he could not be interred at the graveyard, but Anne scattered her son's ashes there. She committed suicide in 1996. Before she died, she is said to have confessed that she purposely administered another dose of heroin to her son, possibly to save him from going to prison.

Despite Vicious' death and the Sex Pistols having disbanded, their music continued to be popular. The four original members of the Sex Pistols, Lydon, Jones, Cook and Matlock, reunited in 1996. Because of Vicious' drug use, his memory of the night of Spungen's death was unclear. He was never proved to be her murderer. The 2009 film *Who Killed Nancy?* highlights the fact that the couple's money was missing from the apartment where she died. The film suggests that a drug addict who lived at the hotel and had been seen with a wad of cash tied with Spungen's purple hair tie was the killer. Whether Vicious killed Spungen remains debatable.

Another group that came to fame in the 1970s, Thin Lizzy, was also to suffer a casualty when one of its members fell into drug use. Irish musician Phil Lynott co-founded Irish rock band Thin Lizzy in 1969. As the group's lead vocalist, bass guitarist and lyricist, Lynott helped Thin Lizzy become one of the major bands of the late 1970s, writing hit singles including 1976's spectacular 'The Boys are Back in Town', which went on to become an Irish rugby anthem, and 1977's pop classic 'Dancing in the Moonlight (It's Caught Me in its Spotlight)'. Tall and lean with an Afro hairstyle, Lynott's good looks and soft Dublin brogue made him a charismatic frontman. He knew how to work the stage, and Thin Lizzy was regarded as one of the best live rock bands. Off-stage, Lynott embraced the flamboyance of a rock 'n' roll lifestyle, including drink, drugs and groupies, once boasting he had a "chick in every town".

Philip Parris "Phil" Lynott was born in West Bromwich, near Birmingham, in 1949, the illegitimate son of white Irish Catholic Philomena Lynott and Guyanese Cecil Parris. Initially, he was brought up in Moss Side, Manchester, before moving to the Crumlin area of Dublin to live with his maternal grandparents. Of mixed race, Lynott encountered some prejudice while he was growing up. Attracted to music, he joined several rock bands, but it was with Thin Lizzy that he found success.

Thin Lizzy had their first hit in 1972 with a rock version of the traditional Irish folk song 'Whisky in the Jar'. In 1974, Thin Lizzy underwent a series of changes. Guitarist Eric Bell left, to be replaced by Gary Moore, and then when Moore left, guitarists Brian Robertson and Scott Gorham joined. The new line-up with its twin guitar harmonic riffs changed the band's sound and fortune. By 1976, *Melody Maker* was calling Thin Lizzy "the band for thinking rock fans". By 1977, the band had produced the top-selling album *Jailbreak*, done a highly successful American tour supporting Queen, and had headlined the Reading Festival. In August that year, the members of the Dublin-based group were hailed as heroes when they went home to play at a rock festival in the city's Dalymount Park. The band worked hard, partied hard and toured relentlessly. However, in 1979 things took a turn for the worse, as the partying took on a darker element and Lynott acquired a serious drug habit.

However, it looked as if Lynott had calmed down when he married Caroline Crowther, the daughter of TV presenter Leslie Crowther and the mother of his 14-month-old daughter, Sarah, on 14th February, Valentine's Day, 1980. The couple had a second daughter, Cathleen, in July. The one-time wild man seemed to have his mind on other things. He was a devoted father and adored his daughters, even writing songs dedicated to them. He launched a solo career that he pursued in parallel to his Thin Lizzy role. Nevertheless, the rock star still made news, and in June he was treated in hospital for a cut on the face after a punch-up at a party in Southampton. His right eye was damaged and he suffered loss of vision.

A year later, after a long time cultivating one of the wildest wine, women and song images the rock world had ever known, Lynott dismissed the tales of "a new woman a night" as if they had never happened – and even admitted a lot never did. Aged 31, happily married and a father, Lynott appeared tamed, telling the *Daily Mirror*: "People say I'm a different person now. My life has changed, certainly, but that doesn't mean I have. I'm still the same person as far as I'm concerned. All the publicity was very flattering, but not a lot of it was true. If people came to me expecting to hear that kind of thing, and only asked me about the women, that's the picture they got of me." It was an image that stuck to him. He said: "I don't know how all that started really. Perhaps it was the studs and the leather that did it. You know, people thought: 'He wears studs so he must be like that.'" He brushed aside the obvious pressures his image must have put on his relationship with his wife, saying: "Caroline was my publicist before she was my girlfriend – that's how we met – so she always knew what was the image and what was the real me."

That same year, Thin Lizzy released their 12th album and there was talk Lynott would star as one of his heroes, rock guitarist Jimi Hendrix, in a film. Lynott's obvious dedication to work might have almost made him respectable if it had not been for a drugs conviction in August for possession of cocaine, resulting in a £200 fine. He made no comment on the verdict, but attacked what he said were the myths surrounding rock and drugs: "It's just not true that everyone spends all their time taking drugs. So many people have just ruined themselves with them, I would never really get involved."

Lynott was torn between wanting to be a family man and living up to his rock renegade reputation. He was also under pressure to repeat Thin Lizzy's success. Despite stating that he would not ruin his life, he fell back into his self-destructive world of drink and drugs, using cocaine and heroin. By 1982, record sales were falling and he fell deeper into addiction. The drugs sapped his creativity, making him irritable and increasingly difficult to work with. Thin Lizzy decided to split to allow Lynott to pursue his solo career. The band did a farewell tour of Europe that was a sell-out, playing their last concert on 4th September 1983 in Nuremberg, Germany.

The break-up of Thin Lizzy was the beginning of the end for Lynott. He formed a new band, Grand Slam, but it soon collapsed. Lynott's personal life was also troubled. His wife Caroline could not cope with his drug problem and the couple separated in May 1984. Although they were apart, Caroline's love never faltered. There was no talk of divorce and, despite rumours of other women, brave Caroline maintained a dignified silence. She took her daughters to see their father at weekends and tried to help him overcome his drug problems. However, parted from his family and the band that had played such a huge part of his life, Lynott became depressed. Taking drugs and drinking appeared to give him some release from his insecurities but marked the start of a downward spiral. In July 1985, Lynott was charged with possessing cocaine and cannabis. In November 1985, there were rumours that Thin Lizzy would re-form the following March. Lynott had achieved only modest success in his solo career and his management admitted: "They are very much in touch again." However, Lynott died before any reunion could happen.

A girlfriend of Lynott's, Heather Mitson, approached the *Daily Mirror* before Christmas 1985, feeling that by making his drug and alcohol problems public, she would shock him into giving up drugs. Published after Lynott's death, Mitson's interview paints a picture of the rock star's tragic decline in the months leading up to it. Mitson said: "Phil was everything I had ever imagined about rock stars. He lived the legend to the full. Everywhere he went he was driven in limousines. We ate in the best restaurants and his house was like a palace. Phil was famous and everyone wanted to be his friend." She continued: "When we first met we had the most fantastic time together. We loved and kissed and laughed and partied all night. But there's difference between sipping the finest vintage champagne, and getting stoned on a bottle of brandy for a breakfast."

Mitson explained how Lynott changed after Thin Lizzy broke up: "Sadly, he could never face the fact that his days with Thin Lizzy were over. He had a juke box in his house, and every song was a Thin Lizzy record ... It was as if he was desperately clinging onto his former glory." She said Lynott was "a perfect victim for heroin" and used it to kill his misery: "Phil just couldn't cope with seeing all that was his slip away from him. He was no longer quite so famous or quite so glamorous. He went through an agony of self-doubt and self-hate. I watched him go from bad to worse. I begged Phil to sort himself out, but heroin already had its grip on him. Drugs were his only release from the pain of being Phil Lynott."

Mitson said Lynott had chosen to spend more time with friends who shared his drug habit. She described the atmosphere at Lynott's big house by Kew Gardens – the house where his slide into drug addiction was to enter its final phase: "Phil kept a string of hangers-on at his house whose sole purpose was to reassure him he was wonderful, fetch him drugs, and feed him. They turned his beautiful home into a squalid dump with cigarette stubs, dirty dishes and stale food strewn everywhere."

Mitson saw him less and less as Lynott began to seek the company of fellow addicts. By then, he was drinking a bottle of brandy a day. She recalled: "I'll never forget a show at St Austell in Cornwall. He had taken a lot of heroin and pushed a fan on to the pavement, bruising him badly. He went berserk if anyone dared to speak to him. I was standing on one of the theatre balconies and when he saw me he tried to push me over. He'd completely taken leave of his senses. Heroin had turned him into a monster. Almost every day I asked him to go to a clinic for help and have a doctor sort him out. But he would say that he was a famous pop star, and pop stars were supposed to take drugs. I tried everything to make him understand that I loved him too much to see him destroy himself. But he had already reached the point of no return."

Finally, Mitson realized how bad things really were when they were making love at his house one night: "We were very close and tender when Phil broke away. He was fumbling beneath the bed for something. Suddenly I realised he was sticking a needle full of heroin into his arm. I was so revolted, I leapt out of bed, pulled my clothes on, and fled." Mitson never saw Lynott again.

On 4th January 1986, Lynott died at the age of 35 after years of drug abuse. Lynott had collapsed from a drink and drug binge on Christmas Day at his home in Kew. His mother discovered him but did not know of her son's heroin habit – he had been injecting himself in the feet. Initially, she thought he had a stomach bug and then a friend of her son arrived at the house and explained he needed help. She telephoned Lynott's estranged 27-year-old wife, Caroline, who dashed 100 miles to his rescue. At the inquest into Lynott's death Caroline said: "As soon as I saw him I realised he was unwell and thought it was due to drugs."

Lynott feebly asked her for help. Immediately, before he changed his mind, Caroline contacted a clinic in Wiltshire that specialized in drugs and alcohol dependency, which agreed to admit him. Unable to walk and barely able to talk, he was carried out to a vehicle by two friends and driven to the clinic. At the inquest, the clinic's resident medical director said Lynott arrived at 7.30pm. He was unable to stand and was semi-comatose. Later, when the doctor went to his room, Lynott was lucid, but very weak. His blood pressure was low, his temperature was up and he was sweating profusely. There was a swelling to his right elbow that appeared to be septic. His system was failing and he needed to get to a hospital.

Lynott was transferred to the nearest hospital, Salisbury Infirmary, where he was put into intensive care. His condition worsened and he was put on a respirator. Lynott's mother, wife and father-in-law kept vigil at his hospital bedside. After fighting for his life, Lynott died of pneumonia and heart failure due to sepsis. Sadly, Caroline lost a race against time to be with him on the day he died, reaching his bedside just 15 minutes too late. Her last loving gesture moved the coroner at the subsequent inquest to say: "I would like to commend the action of a caring wife who tried so hard, but failed, to save his life." Caroline wept silently as the coroner added: "What a waste of a talented life. I hope his death may be a warning to those who are thinking of taking hard drugs under the impression they are not dangerous. Make no mistake – they are lethal." The pathologist at the inquest revealed that there were numerous abscesses in the rock star's heart, kidney and spleen, and bacteria had been growing in the blood. The cause of death was multiple abscesses due to septicaemia, probably brought about by injecting drugs. The coroner recorded that Lynott died from drug dependency.

At the time of his death, Lynott was involved in various music projects and working on a new album. Many remember Lynott for his considerable creative talent, intelligence and culture. He is also recalled with affection as one of the nicest men in the music business, known for being smart, funny, generous and terrific company. Lynott was the driving force behind Thin Lizzy, which paved the way for Irish band U2, and he was the first black Irish rock star. On stage, Lynott was a dynamic rocker, worshipped by a generation of fans. Yet, in his final days, the former Thin Lizzy frontman was a shambling, decaying wreck, destroyed by drugs as the excesses of his lifestyle finally caught up with him. In an interview for the VH1 TV documentary *Behind the Music* on Thin Lizzy in 1999, Lynott's mother said she was haunted by her son's music, recalling the lines of 'Old Town' from *The Philip Lynott Album*, released in 1982: "This boy is cracking up / This boy has broken down." She said: "Every time I hear it he was saying something but nobody listened." Lynott's catalogue of work continues to inspire musicians and, in 2005, a bronze statue of Lynott was erected in Dublin in his memory.

Kurt Cobain made his name on America's grunge music scene as Nirvana's lead singer, guitarist and main songwriter. He became a star after the release of the band's 10 million-selling album *Nevermind* in 1991. The cynical image on the album cover of a baby swimming after a dollar bill suspended from a fishing hook as if in the pursuit of money became immortalized in rock history. A surprise hit, *Nevermind* became a landmark album for the so-called "Generation X". Inspired by heavy metal, punk and indie rock, grunge music became mainstream thanks to Nirvana, and Cobain was hailed as its king. The star was regarded as a spokesman for a generation – a role he disdained. The pressure and publicity surrounding Nirvana's success took its toll on the young man, who suffered from depression and a debilitating medical condition that saw him self-medicate by turning to heroin. The shy and reserved Cobain appeared a reluctant rock star dazed by his band's commercial success.

Born in Aberdeen, Washington, in 1967, Cobain's mother was a waitress and his father a car mechanic. His parents divorced when he was eight years old; his father subsequently remarried. Cobain later admitted that he felt resentful towards his family, becoming withdrawn and angry. Interested in music and art, when Cobain got a guitar for his 14th birthday he found solace in music. A rebellious teenager, he began dabbling in drugs. In 1985, Cobain was arrested for spray painting buildings, receiving a fine and suspended sentence. He found himself in trouble again a year later, when he was discovered wandering drunk in an abandoned building at night, and spent a few days in jail.

Cobain found an outlet for his creativity, anger and dysfunction when he formed Nirvana in 1987 with friend and bassist Krist Novoselic. They released their first album, *Bleach*, in June 1989. The band went through a series of drummers until Dave Grohl joined the line-up in 1990. Nirvana's raw energy, sense of fun and refreshing integrity, combined with a healthy cynicism regarding the music industry, found a fan base. But already all was not well with the young Cobain. In September 1990, rock photographer Ian Tilton famously photographed him backstage sobbing after a gig in Seattle. Interviewed later about the iconic shot, which is unusual in showing a star's vulnerability, Tilton said of Cobain: "He simply came off stage, sat down and cried for about half a minute. Then he was fine. He had just trashed his gear on stage, and it was simply a release of energy. It is a painful picture, but it's about the angst of performance. The band seemed used to it. He seemed very healthy then, and very happy. He was a very powerful and energetic performer, and it was all he wanted to do. The band was his vehicle, the most important thing in his life."

By then, Cobain had developed a heroin addiction. He suffered from an undiagnosed stomach complaint and was in chronic pain, later claiming that he started using heroin regularly in order to alleviate it. The "recurrent burning stomach pain" was thought to be connected to psychological problems stemming from the break-up of his parents' marriage. The combination of a medical condition and addiction did not bode well for the sensitive Cobain, who was soon to discover what it felt like to be famous. Nirvana signed a deal with Geffen Records in 1991, *Nevermind* ensued and, with it, the hit single 'Smells Like Teen Spirit'. Suddenly, the band and Cobain were an international success. They acquired a reputation as wild rockers because of their antics on stage, smashing up equipment at the end of gigs. During the 1991 European tour to promote the album, the group's wrecking spree cost thousands of pounds. The band smashed up two backstage dressing rooms and set fire to their tour bus after a sold-out gig in Germany. Cobain admitted: "I set fire to the curtains while I was being interviewed on the tour bus and the whole place filled up with smoke." A spokesman for the band said: "The band makes a habit of smashing things up. Their behaviour is costing us a fortune."

That same year, Cobain began dating Hole guitarist and singer, Courtney Love. Known for her unpredictable and outrageous behaviour – as well as her bouts of drink and drug abuse – Love is a controversial figure. The couple took drugs together. Love's relationship with Cobain provoked mixed reactions from both Cobain's fans and the media. The couple married

in Hawaii in February 1992, when Love was pregnant with their child.
In March, Nirvana cancelled two shows in Australia during their Pacific
Rim tour, saying that Cobain had caught a stomach bug. When the band
got back on the road, the Seattle star said: "We've been under a lot
of pressure."

Before going on tour to Australia and New Zealand, Cobain had
entered rehab in an attempt to tackle his drug addiction. He then suffered
withdrawal symptoms during the tour. In an interview in 1993, Cobain
discussed his stomach ailment, drugs and how he felt as Nirvana hit the big
time: "I was in pain for so long that I didn't care if I was in a band. I didn't
care if I was alive, and it just so happened that I came to that conclusion at
a time when my band became really popular … It had been going on and
building up for so many years that I was suicidal. I just didn't want to live. I
just thought if I'm going to die, if I'm going to kill myself I should take some
drugs. I may as well become a junkie as I felt like a junkie every day. Waking
up starving, forcing myself to eat, barfing it back up … I'm in pain all the
time and being on tour it was a lot worse, it made it even worse."

In March 1992, Cobain sought to change Nirvana's agreement
regarding royalties to reflect the fact he wrote the majority of
songs. Until then, the proceeds were split equally between Cobain,
Novoselic and Grohl. Cobain wanted a 100 per cent share of the
lyrics and 75 per cent of the music – he also wanted the agreement
to be applied retroactively to *Nevermind*. Eventually, his fellow band
members agreed, but Cobain's request led to tension within the
group. Rumours began to circulate that Nirvana might disband.

There were tensions in Cobain's personal life too. Love gave birth to their daughter, Frances Bean, in August. However, a month later, the couple went from being the new John and Yoko to being America's most reviled couple after Love was interviewed by journalist Lynn Hirschberg for magazine *Vanity Fair*. The article reported that Love went on a drugs binge while she was pregnant. Love denied the allegations, later saying she consulted doctors as soon as she found out she was pregnant and then went into rehab. However, the Los Angeles County Department of Children's Services took the couple to court, claiming that their drug use made them unfit parents. Two weeks after their daughter was born, a judge ordered the removal of the baby from their custody. Love's sister, Jamie, took care of the child. Cobain and his wife went berserk. It took months of legal wrangling before the couple gained full custody of their daughter and they had to submit to regular urine tests. Later Love said: "It was totally crazy and really freaked us out. After Frances was born a social worker walked into my room with a picture from *Vanity Fair* and tried to take her away."

In September, a month after Frances Bean was born, Nirvana played at the MTV Video Music Awards in Los Angeles. Cobain caused thousands of pounds of damage by smashing his guitar, wrecking an amplifier and falling on a drum kit. The group picked up awards for Best Alternative Video and Best New Artist in a Video for 'Smells Like Teen Spirit'. Despite his stint in rehab, Cobain started using heroin again after he got back from touring the Pacific. His habit is reported to have cost him $400 a day, and that it was sufficiently serious for one dealer in Seattle to be so afraid the star would overdose that he refused to sell to him anymore.

Cobain's life seemed to be out of control. In October, he threatened journalists writing an unauthorized book on Nirvana. He wanted to stop Irish rock journalist Victoria Clarke and her colleague Britt Collins from publishing the book, set to reveal intimate details about the band and his wife. Cobain left a message on Clarke's answering machine saying: "At this point I don't give a flying fuck if I have this recorded that I'm threatening you. I suppose I could throw out a few thousand dollars to have you snuffed out, but maybe I'll try the legal way. First." Clarke told *Select* magazine: "Kurt and Courtney have a lot of money and are very intimidating."

In December, Nirvana released a compilation album *Incesticide*. Copies of the original sleeve notes included a rambling letter from Cobain. The sleeve notes were not included on final copies of the album because of time and printing constraints, even though Cobain had insisted they be included. In the notes, Cobain raged against the author of the *Vanity Fair* article and the authors of the unofficial Nirvana biography: "I think it's very sad that we can't move onward in the history/demise of rock music instead of assigning me/us/my wife these ridiculous, archetypal, retro, rock roles to live out. We are decent, ethical people – we take no delight in being involved in blatant sexism, treachery, or scandals made up off the top of someone's head … we are having to deal with the betrayal and harassment that stems from the 'inside sources' and aspiring groupie 'writer', who surround us now like celebrity-worshipping jackals moving in for the kill."

One pressing of the album contains notes where Cobain sarcastically describes receiving a copy of the out-of-print first Raincoats LP with the band members' signatures. His self-loathing, hatred of the music industry and dislike of the trappings of fame is evident as he says obtaining a copy of the classic vinyl LP made him happier than "playing in front of thousands of people each night, rock-god idolization from fans, music industry plankton kissing my ass, and the million dollars I made last year. It was one of the most important things that I've been blessed with since becoming an untouchable boy genius." He continued: "A big 'fuck you' to those of you who have the audacity to claim that I'm so naïve and stupid that I would allow myself to be taken advantage of and manipulated. I don't feel the least bit guilty for commercially exploiting a completely exhausted Rock youth Culture because, at this point in rock history, Punk Rock (while still sacred to some) is, to me, dead and gone."

Cobain also addressed proclaimed Nirvana fans, revealing his resentment against those who did not recognize the band's social and political views: "At this point, I have a request for our fans. If any of you in any way hate homosexuals, people of different color, or women, please do this one favour for us – leave us the fuck alone! Don't come to our shows, and don't buy our records." He signed the letter "Love, Kurdt (the blond one)".

Cobain was struggling to cope with the attention he and his band received as the result of their success, becoming increasingly suspicious of the media. He threw himself into work projects that would challenge his audience. In January 1993, a collaboration between Cobain and his hero, American writer William S. Burroughs, 'The "Priest" They Called Him', was released. It tells the story of a heroin addict trying to get a fix. Cobain had laid down a guitar track the previous November to accompany a reading by Burroughs. The recording fuelled rumours about Cobain's drug use.

Cobain later told journalist Laurence Romance that rumours did not bother him because his heroin use was no longer a secret: "I really don't care what anyone thinks about my past drug use, I mean, I'm definitely not trying to glorify it in any way ... I just thought it was one of those things that you do to relieve the pain, but ... As I expected before I started doing heroin ... I knew at the beginning that it would become just as boring as marijuana does. All drugs, after a few months, it's just as boring as breathing air. I've always lied about it because I never wanted to influence anybody, I didn't want anyone to consider the thought of doing drugs because it's really stupid."

The grunge star's obsession with guns became public in June 1993, when he was hauled off to jail after police were called to a disturbance at his luxury home in Seattle. The incident occurred after neighbours complained about the noise coming from a massive jam session being held at his house. However, when police arrived they found Cobain in the middle of a huge row with his wife – and he was arrested for possible domestic assault. He was released without charge. A police spokesman said: "Washington law states that officers called to a domestic dispute must arrest one of the people involved."

Police described the argument as being over the presence of guns Cobain had recently bought in the house. Love said she did not want guns in the house. Police took three guns into safekeeping, a Beretta .380, a Taurus .380 and a Colt AR-15, as well as ammunition clips for the guns. Love denied that her husband had assaulted her, but said they got into a pushing match. She told the *Seattle Times*: "Kurt is not violent, he is not a wife-beater, we are the most compatible people on earth."

That summer Cobain's health improved when a doctor diagnosed the cause of his stomach pain as a pinched nerve relating to his scoliosis – a curve in the spine – so it then became treatable. However, he was no longer able to excuse away his drug addiction. In August, in an interview with Laurence Romance, he said he longed for a life out of the spotlight: "I would prefer to be a cult act, because cult bands seem to have a very steady lifestyle. They don't have the hassles of being a celebrity …"

In September, Nirvana released its album *In Utero*. Cobain joked of naming it "I Hate Myself and I Want to Die". Some of its songs were seen as his attempt to reconcile himself with fame and the public's interest in his personal life. He denied it. However, he did complain about money. He had spent more than £1 million that year – but did not know what on, saying: "People think because we've sold millions of records we must be set up for life. But it's not the case. I shelled out … on a house … taxes, I lent my mum some money and I bought a car. Now there's nothing left."

Nirvana set off on American and European tours to promote *In Utero* but the European leg was cancelled when, on 5th March 1994, Cobain fell into a coma after a drinks and drug overdose in Rome. Cobain's wife, Love, raised the alarm when she woke up to find he had collapsed in their luxury hotel suite, where they were staying with their daughter on a short break between concert dates. Cobain was rushed to hospital in a coma at 6.30am, where doctors worked for five hours to save him from the potentially lethal mixture of barbiturates and booze. Doctors pumped his stomach but his condition remained "grave". Cobain emerged from the coma in the afternoon. Love then had her husband moved across the city to an American private hospital amid a clampdown on information about his condition. The incident showed that although he had pledged to stop taking drugs when his daughter was born and claimed he had beaten his heroin habit, he was still addicted.

Later, Love revealed that Cobain had left a suicide note and his overdose was not accidental. The couple scrapped their April tours as doctors ordered Cobain to rest at home in Seattle. However, they still argued about his drug use and, on 18th March, Love called the police to report that Cobain was suicidal. He had locked himself in a room at their home in Seattle with a .38-calibre revolver. Cobain insisted he was not suicidal and the police recovered the gun. Love told the police he had not said he was suicidal, but she knew he had access to guns and was worried. She staged an intervention in an attempt to get him off drugs. He went to a chemical dependency clinic in Los Angeles but left after a few days.

On 8th April, Cobain was found dead. The scene of the rock legend's last act was tragically squalid. A million miles from the glitz of pop stardom, the tortured hero shot himself dead in the greenhouse above his garage at his home in Lake Washington, Seattle. Detectives were called to the singer's home by an electrician, who found the body after arriving to do wiring work. As the police went through the back door in pouring rain, they discovered a shocking sight. Cobain's skinny body lay spreadeagled across the kitchen floor, with a sole spent gun cartridge nearby on the tobacco-coloured linoleum. At his side were a discarded computer game, music cassettes and a copy of *In Utero*. Next to them was what appeared to be a battered olive-green cuddly toy.

Twenty-seven-year-old Cobain was dressed, as always, in scruffy blue jeans and sneakers – the rebellious uniform which made him "Godfather of Grunge" and an idol to millions of teenagers. Troubled Cobain, a cripplingly shy man who became the reluctant voice of a generation, had blasted himself through the head. He left a suicide note. He wrote: "I haven't felt the excitement of listening to as well as creating music along with reading and writing for too many years now. I feel guilty beyond words about these things. For example when we're backstage and the lights go out and the manic roar of the crowd begins, it doesn't affect me the way in which it did for Freddie Mercury, who seem to love, relish in the love and adoration from the crowd, which is something I totally admire and envy. The fact is, I can't fool you, any one of you. It simply isn't fair to you or me. The worst crime I can think of would be to rip people off by faking it and pretending as if I'm having 100% fun. Sometimes I feel as if I should have a punch-in time clock before I walk out on stage. I've tried everything within my power to appreciate it (and I do, God believe me I do, but it's not enough). I appreciate the fact that I and we have affected and entertained a lot of people. I must be one of those narcissists who only appreciate things when they're gone. I'm too sensitive. I need to be slightly numb in order to regain the enthusiasm I once had as a child. On our last 3 tours, I've had a much better appreciation for all the people I've known personally, and as fans of our music, but I still can't get over the frustration, the guilt and empathy I have for everyone. There's good in all of us and I think I simply love people too much, so much that it makes me feel too fucking sad. The sad little, sensitive, unappreciative, Pisces, Jesus man. Why don't you just enjoy it? I don't know! I don't know! I have a goddess of a wife who sweats ambition and empathy and a daughter who reminds me too much of what I used to be, full of love and joy, kissing every person she meets because everyone is good and will do her no harm. And that terrifies me to the point where I can barely function. I can't stand the thought of Frances becoming the miserable, self-destructive, death rocker that I've become. I have it good, very good, and I'm grateful, but since the age of seven, I've become hateful towards all humans in general. Only because it seems so easy for people to get along and have empathy. Only because I love and feel sorry for people too much I guess. Thank you all from the pit of my burning, nauseous stomach for your letters and concern during the past years. I'm too much of an erratic, moody, baby! I don't have the passion anymore, and so remember, it's better to burn out than to fade away."

The note ended with a scrawled message to his wife and daughter: "I love you, I love you."

Friends admitted that Cobain's death had come as no surprise. He could no longer cope with the pressures of fame. A friend of Cobain's told the *Daily Mirror*: "He was in despair. He'd tried all sorts of ways of kicking the junk but he kept slipping back. It was his way of dealing with it all – by disappearing up a needle. He was always fascinated by suicide, always messing about posing with guns in his mouth and saying life would be easier if he just died. When I heard the news, I just thought 'He's finally gone and done it.'"

The Seattle Police Department incident report stated that Cobain was found with a shotgun across his body and a visible head wound. The police concluded that Cobain had committed suicide and estimated he had died on 5th April. There were puncture wounds on the inside of both the right and left elbow. Toxicology reports revealed he had heroin and diazepam in his blood.

Conspiracy theories regarding his possible murder followed, and some even suggested his wife had been involved. The police have not reopened the case. Love fell into drug abuse for a period and in later years became estranged from her daughter. Nirvana released *Unplugged in New York* shortly after Cobain's death and it went to the top of the charts. A lengthy battle between Grohl, Novoselic and Love over Nirvana's music was resolved in 2002, paving the way for a new album, which included previously unreleased material. In 2006, Cobain beat Elvis Presley to become the world's top-earning dead celebrity. Presley reclaimed the spot a year later.

Almost as soon as Cobain died, he was hailed as a "rock god", a tag often attached to those who die young. However, unlike Bob Marley, Jimi Hendrix and Jim Morrison, Cobain's death was no accident: he committed suicide in a fit of deep depression. A cousin of his claimed that Cobain was bipolar, pointing out that two uncles had also committed suicide with guns. Cobain and Nirvana helped make alternative rock go mainstream, spearheading the way for bands like Pearl Jam. The blue-eyed blonde musician appeared too frail to handle fame, but, ironically, his early demise helped guarantee his iconic status in rock history.

Addiction is not the sole domain of rock musicians. Many in the public life, from actors to athletes, have adopted a fast-living lifestyle of sex. When a sportsman famed for his athleticism falls by the wayside it somehow seems worse. Their health and physical prowess is part of their appeal. One of the saddest victims of fame is Irish football player George Best. He was a teenage football sensation, but his later love of women, booze and a playboy lifestyle saw the footballing genius pushed out of Manchester United. While Best's considerable talent on the pitch is in no doubt and meant he was revered in his lifetime, he made headlines as much for his struggle with alcohol addiction as for his skill. Feted when he died of organ failure aged 59, his past escapades were forgiven by fans who adored him. Nevertheless, Best was an alcoholic for longer than he was a great footballer. His alcoholism ruined both his career and his life.

Best was born in Belfast in 1946 into a Protestant family. He inherited his sporting ability from his mother, Anne, who was a talented hockey player. A teetotaller until she was in her 40s, Anne died of alcoholism in 1978 aged 54. A talent scout for Manchester United spotted Best when he was 15 and soon the young Best was far from home in a city he did not know. In 1962, United's legendary manager, Sir Matt Busby, signed Best as a 16-year-old. Best went on to make 470 appearances and score 179 goals for the club. He won two league titles at Old Trafford but the high point of his career came in 1968, when he scored a superb goal against Benfica to help United to lift the European Cup. The same year, Best won Football Writers' Footballer of the Year and European Footballer of the Year.

Best made his debut for Northern Ireland at the age of 17 and played 37 games for the side until 1977. His talent shone brightest during the late 1960s and early 1970s, when the Troubles in Northern Ireland were at their peak. He made Belfast famous for more than violence, and crowds loved him for it. Best understood he was the property of all Irishmen, and friends said they never heard him utter a word about religion or politics.

Good-looking and determined, Best was football's first superstar. He trained and trained to improve his left foot in a way few footballers can be bothered to do. Off the field, he was astute, funny, charming and a ladies' man, known for dating beauty queens, actresses and models. However, as Best's career took off, he started to hit the booze and made headlines for outings with beautiful women and evenings in nightclubs. He began to get in trouble: he had problems behaving on the pitch and turned up late for training. In the beginning, his indulgences were overlooked by a club in awe of his talent. Then, in 1971, he was fined a record £250 by the Football Association for receiving three yellow cards for misconduct. The fine and a suspended sentence of six weeks followed three cautions in 12 months. Best did not learn a lesson and, only days afterwards, he missed the train taking his team to London for a game with Chelsea.

Best continued to make headlines for his off-pitch antics and no-shows on it. By 1972, the press feared he was unable to cope adequately with fame and dubbed him the "wandering superstar". He appeared to have lost his appetite for football and his brilliance dimmed. As he caused United problems – on and off the field – fans and the press began to talk of the unthinkable: the club selling Best.

Speculation mounted that Best was thinking of quitting the game that built him into a star – and he did. In May 1972, on holiday in Marbella in Spain, he stressed there was absolutely no going back on his decision. He told the *Daily Mirror*: "I can live quite comfortably off my investments. But

I don't want to be a bum – I want to work." Looking tired and drawn, he added: "Money just doesn't interest me." Beside the swimming pool of a five-star hotel, the man who had the football world at his feet went on: "I won't change my mind – I've played my last game."

Then, as he sipped an iced beer, Best talked of the nights when he took to drink: "I have been drunk several times, but never incapable. For two years, I have not been able to sleep properly. I have gone to bed at 2am and got up two hours later just to have a drink, in the hope that it would get me off to sleep. It would take me nine months of very hard work to get even physically fit again. Now I am going away for six months – anywhere. I have finished with the Manchester scene."

However, Best did return to Manchester and continued to play for United. His no-shows continued and in 1974, at the age of 27, he quit the club for good. After leaving, he admitted to drinking vast amounts of brandy and champagne to give him a "buzz". He returned to football for a number of clubs around the world for short spells, but his glory days were over and he played for anyone who would pay him. The stories and the headlines about Best featured football less and less. They were all about birds, booze and bankruptcy. He finally retired in 1983, age 37.

Best's drinking also affected his domestic life. He married his first wife, Angie Janes, a model, in 1978, and they had a son, Calum, in 1981. Best vainly joined Alcoholics Anonymous but neither it nor family life managed to curb his drinking. In December 1984, he hit rock bottom when he was sentenced to three months in jail for a drink-driving offence, assaulting a police officer and failing to appear in court. The Bow Street court heard that Best failed to appear there in November for a drink-driving charge. He then scuffled with police who went to arrest him, punching one in a police van near his Chelsea home. A defence lawyer explained that Best had not turned up at court because he had overslept – through drink. Best was sent to London's Pentonville Prison and later transferred to Ford Open Prison in West Sussex to finish his sentence. There he appeared for his final team – Ford Open Prison. In 1984, Best and Angie divorced, although they remained friends. By 1988, with Best facing bankruptcy, friends organized a testimonial on his behalf and raised £75,000.

By the 1990s, Best was on medication to stop drinking. In 1995, he married 23-year-old air hostess Alex Pursey. Three years later, he joined Sky Sports as a pundit. However, the same year Best was forced to move out of his Chelsea home after allegations he was £70,000 in arrears on the mortgage. Then came the inevitable blow. In 2000, he was diagnosed with severe liver damage. He was admitted to hospital, coughing up blood. Best said of the crisis: "I was dying. You can't go any lower than that."

Best stayed sober for a year and had Antabuse anti-alcohol pellets inserted into his stomach – the tablets cause nausea and vomiting if alcohol is taken. He convinced doctors he had earned the right to a new liver and had a transplant on the National Health Service in 2002. There was an outcry in the press because many were vehemently opposed to him receiving NHS treatment due to the fact he was an alcoholic. His surgeon revealed he had been on the brink of organ failure before the operation and that without a new liver he would have died, possibly in three months. Best hit back at critics who said his boozy lifestyle was not worth saving:

"I didn't decide one day that I would drink myself to death. Alcoholism is a disease. I wouldn't say to anybody that they don't deserve to live, no matter who they are." The wayward former footballer was warned that he must never drink again as he continued with the implant treatment. Best swore he would never touch another drink in respect for the unknown organ donor who gave him the gift of life. It appeared he must have convinced the public and the media as he won the BBC Sports Personality of the Year Lifetime Achievement Award in 2002.

Only a year later, reports appeared in the media saying Best was back indulging in drinking binges and affairs. Not even the precious second chance given to him by the transplant could stop him going back to the bottle. He was so down on his luck that he sold his European Footballer of the Year award for £150,000. In July, he was arrested after a brawl with a photographer at the Chequers pub in Walton-on-the-Hill, Surrey. He was released without charge and went straight back to the Chequers. Regulars at the Chequers confirmed he was downing scotch and brandy on the night of the brawl. The landlord of the Chequers pub vowed not to sell him any more alcohol. Meanwhile, an enterprising butcher opposite the pub put up a sign saying "Best Liver Sold Here". Best was a laughing stock.

Once more, Best vowed to kick alcohol for good, admitting one of the problems he faced was terrible mood swings and cravings for booze: "At times I get terribly depressed. I will probably have to go on Prozac but I also want to give my days a little more structure ... I'll have new Antabuse sewn into my stomach in September and hope they'll work. I'm taking drastic action. My willpower alone just won't do it. In my weaker moments I know my craving could get the better of me."

That summer, Best publicly fell off the wagon. He attacked a photographer while holidaying in Corfu with his wife Alex. He also admitted kissing a woman, who he met in his local pub in Surrey, but claimed he had been set up. Asked why he had let himself descend into boozing again on a donated liver, he replied sharply: "I don't care what people think about me drinking. That's no one else's business."

In December, it was evident how low the football legend had fallen when Best confessed he had been ripped off by two whores in a Fulham hotel room, saying: "I thought they were nice enough girls." The same month he was blamed for a slump in organ donors. According to surgeons, his binge drinking after he was given a new liver had a devastating effect on transplant waiting lists.

In January 2004, Alex called time on their marriage after allegedly receiving a beating from Best on Boxing Day that left her covered in cuts and bruises. She refused to press charges but later divorced him on grounds of adultery. Best continued to spiral and was banned from driving for 20 months for drink-driving. Various TV documentaries aired about him, including *The Truth about George Best*, in which he agreed to take part. His father Dick, sister Barbara and son Calum excused his unreliability and dependence on alcohol. His ex-wife Angie said it was like being married to an angel and the devil at the same time. He had been told alcohol, and brandy in particular, would destroy his new liver. Asked how long it had been since his last brandy, Best said: "About twelve hours."

On 1st October 2005, Best was admitted to Cromwell Hospital in London with flu-like symptoms, but deteriorated rapidly after he developed a kidney infection and was moved into intensive care. For the next two weeks, he battled infections and prolonged bouts of internal bleeding. He rallied and was thought to be improving. Then he developed a lung infection and was put on a ventilator in intensive care. He fell unconscious and died on 25th November. Just days earlier, a photograph appeared in the press showing him in his hospital bed along with his message: "Don't die like me."

Best's death certificate showed he lost his life to a shocking list of illnesses. He had "pneumonia, septicaemia, gastrointestinal bleeding and multi-organ failure". A secondary cause was "immuno-suppression following liver transplant". He had requested his body parts to be used for transplants. His wish could not be granted because of the state of his organs. He died unable to pay medical fees thought to top £100,000. Doctors at the Cromwell are believed to have waived payment.

Belfast gave the city's most famous football son what verged on a state funeral, granting him the kind of dignity that eluded him for much of his life. Hundreds of thousands lined the streets of Belfast to say farewell. The funeral service was held at Stormont, Northern Ireland's palatial parliament building. The flags over Stormont fluttered at half-mast, an occurrence reserved for royalty. Sinn Fein's Martin McGuinness and the Progressive Unionist Party's David Irvine left the funeral service side by side. Some 30,000 people braved the rain to pay their last respects when Best was buried at Roselawn Cemetery. To many, the fact that Best managed to be continuously drunk for the last 30 years of his life yet always had a pretty blonde on his arm made him the personification of an impossibly glamorous dream. Best's friend and United team-mate, Paddy Crerand, said every man wanted to live like him.

Not everyone felt so generous towards Best: some attributed a lack of donors for liver swap operations to his behaviour. The controversy did not wane. In 2006, a mother whose five-year-old daughter would die without a new liver blamed "the George Best effect" for a critical shortage of donors. The British Organ Donor Society said although the number of liver donors actually increased when Best was given his liver transplant, later, when he continued boozing and died in November, the figures fell. A spokesman for the society said: "It's a shame to let any prejudice get in the way of people making donations. George Best himself wanted to donate his organs and that was the message he gave from his death bed."

As a footballer Best was sublime, as a man he was tragically flawed. While warning youngsters not to drink themselves into an early grave, he remained unrepentant about the booze-sodden path he had trodden. "I wouldn't change a thing about my life," he said. "Women, booze, gambling – I'd do exactly the same again." Next to his few fleeting years of glory, there was another side to him: the hopeless drunk, absent father and wife beater. However, he remains idolized. On the first anniversary of Best's death, a million £5 notes showing him in his Manchester United and Northern Ireland strips were issued as a tribute. When the notes were released, there were queues outside Ulster Bank branches across Northern Ireland, and every note was snapped up. In 2013, Best featured on a set of stamps to celebrate 150 years of the Football Association, and all stamped mail posted to Belfast had a special "George Best" postmark. Best remains one of football's iconic players. Fans remember him with gratitude for his skill and sadness for his failings.

There are no conspiracy theories around Best's death, unlike those of many other stars. The heady mix of fame, drink, drugs and sex lends itself to such stories. Perhaps with good reason – fame brings money, power and envy with it. Together, they can be a toxic recipe for dark deeds. Perhaps fans do not want to let their idols go and are ever searching for a reason why those who soared so high plummeted so low and crashed, never to return. Of course, a star's death spawns an industry just as much as when they are alive – through biographies, tributes, films and documentaries – because their memory and achievements become pieces of merchandise. They need to remain alive in people's minds, to be saleable. A death shrouded in mystery adds to their aura.

CHAPTER FIVE:

NOTORIOUS NIGHTMARES

Celebrity turns into notoriety when someone commits a criminal act. When such individuals do not pay for their crimes while they are alive, all that is left is their damaged reputation. Perhaps that is scant comfort to their victims. When a person gets away with exploiting their fame to mask their dirty tricks, the role of the media and the Establishment is questioned – how did they fail to spot and report the crimes? Those who have looked up to people because of their power, wealth, privilege or talent are left reeling in disgust. Suddenly, the idea of 15 minutes of fame loses its appeal because it is clear that celebrity status is no guarantee of honesty or decency.

In Britain, aristocrats enjoy the privilege and sometimes wealth that goes with their position. Providing a touch of old-world glamour, today's media still reports on their lives. So in 1974, when playboy peer Richard

FALLEN IDOLS

John Bingham, popularly known as Lord Lucan, disappeared after the murder of his children's nanny – he was suspected to be her killer – it caused a sensation. The media and the public asked how did an aristocratic family, with fabulous homes and wealth beyond the dreams of most, find themselves at the centre of a horrific murder.

Lord Lucan was born in 1934 into one of Britain's most aristocratic families. Previous earls had held high-profile roles in politics and the military – his great-grandfather was in command when the Light Brigade made their historic charge during the Crimean War. In 1963, he married former model Veronica Duncan. When his father died in 1964, he became the 7th Earl of Lucan. A year later, the Lucans had daughter Frances, followed in 1967 by George and, in 1970, Camilla. An Old Etonian, former Coldstream Guards officer and one-time merchant banker, who drove an Aston Martin, Lucan became part of the international jet set. A bobsleigh enthusiast, powerboat racer and keen golfer, Lord Lucan cut a dashing figure. He was once chosen, for his "English good looks", to star opposite Shirley MacLaine in the film *Woman Times Seven* but he failed a screen test. That failure later led him to turn down an offer by film producer "Cubby" Broccoli to screen-test him for the role of James Bond.

However, behind the veil of glamour all was not well. Despite an initially happy marriage, Lord and Lady Lucan's relationship foundered. Lord Lucan lived the high life: nice clothes, cars and boats, drinking clubs and what would become most important in later life – the friendship of a group of wealthy and powerful men including John Aspinall and Sir James Goldsmith. Lord Lucan was a professional gambler nicknamed "Lucky" – perhaps unkindly given that he racked up massive debts. He regularly gambled at the Clermont Club, founded by Aspinall. The club, at 44 Berkeley Square, was a fashionable casino frequented by rich society figures including politicians, actors, businessmen and aristocrats. Lord Lucan had access to a fortune but he was still living far beyond his means, once even pawning the family silver to pay his gambling debts. He clashed with his young wife who, from a more humble background, feared for the security of her children's future. As the relationship with Lady Lucan broke down, the earl, who did not believe in divorce, tried to get her declared mad by doctors. In order to appease his demands she agreed to take tranquillizers, which gave side effects such as twitching, fuelling rumours of bad health. In 1972, Lord and Lady Lucan separated. Lady Lucan was granted custody of their children. The earl moved out of the family home but he still had to pay his wife a large allowance as well as fund his own lifestyle.

The winter's night of 7th November 1974 started like any other for Lady Lucan. She settled down to watch television with her 10-year-old daughter Frances. Her other children, George and Camilla, had already been put to bed by the family's nanny, 29-year-old Sandra Rivett, who had worked for the Lucans for eight weeks in their home at 46 Lower Belgrave Street in upmarket Belgravia. However, the peace was about to be shattered in a bloody and horrific manner that would leave the married mum-of-one dead and spark one of the biggest manhunts in British criminal history.

The finger quickly pointed to the 39-year-old Lord Lucan, who had a tempestuous relationship with his wife. As far as his family was concerned, he was not at home that night, having moved out in January to live in a flat nearby. He would normally have been at the gaming tables of the casinos around London's Mayfair. What his unsuspecting victims did not know was that he was hiding in the basement of the family home waiting to carry out the chilling murder. The peer intended to batter his wife to death, claiming she was the cause of his tangled financial problems. However, in the darkness he bludgeoned Rivett by mistake, believing she was Lady Lucan.

In the moments before the attack, Rivett had popped her head into Lady Lucan's room and asked if she would like a cup of tea before heading downstairs to make it. At the top of the stairs, the nanny tried to switch on the light but it did not work. Assuming that the bulb had blown – in fact it had been removed – she walked down into the lower floor. In the gloom below, clutching a length of bandaged lead piping, stood Lord Lucan. He had been meticulous in his planning, borrowing a Ford Corsair from a friend, expert backgammon player Michael Stoop, and preparing an alibi at the Clermont Club. However, Lord Lucan could not plan for Rivett changing her evening off at the last minute. As she entered the basement, Lord Lucan struck, raining blow after blow on the defenceless young woman. Her skull was smashed and blood spattered all around. The death was quick and Lord Lucan stuffed the body into a mail sack and calmly walked upstairs, unaware he had killed the wrong person.

Police believe Lord Lucan only realized his mistake when he was disturbed by his wife as she came to look for Rivett, minutes later. Flinging open the bathroom door, he launched a second attack with the piping, this time on the victim he intended. Lady Lucan, barely five feet two and weighing just over seven stone, struggled fiercely with her husband, who forced three gloved fingers down her throat to stop her screaming. Then he tried to strangle her and gouge out one of her eyes. She grabbed his groin, temporarily incapacitating him and making possible her eventual escape. In the inquest into Rivett's death Lady Lucan was asked if her attacker spoke to her and if she recognized the voice. She said: "The person said 'Shut up.' It was my husband."

The pair stopped struggling and went into the bedroom where they saw Frances, who later recounted at the inquest what she recalled. She said: "At about 9.05pm, when the news was on television, daddy and mummy both walked into the room. Mummy had blood on her face and was crying. Mummy told me to go upstairs. After a little while, I don't know how long, because I don't have a clock in my room, I heard daddy calling for mummy. I got up and went to the banisters and looked down and saw daddy coming out of the nursery on the floor below me. He then went into the bathroom on the same floor as the nursery. He came straight out and went downstairs. That was the last I saw of him."

What had in fact happened was Lady Lucan had asked to lie down and, as her husband went to the bathroom to clean blood from himself, she fled into the night to look for help. Police were alerted by a call from the landlord of the nearby Plumbers Arms pub, after Lady Lucan collapsed through the door covered in blood. She cried out: "Help me! I have just escaped from a murderer. My children, my children. He's in my house. He's murdered the nanny. Help me."

In the basement, officers found Rivett's body protruding out of a mailbag, and upstairs they spotted Frances peering through the banisters.

Four-year-old Camilla and seven-year-old George slept through the horrific incident. Meanwhile, Lord Lucan had tried to contact the mother of one of Frances' schoolfriends but she refused to answer her door. Blood was later found on the doorstep. Lord Lucan then called his own mother, asking her to collect the children, before driving to Uckfield in Sussex, where his friends Ian and Susan Maxwell-Scott lived.

Lord Lucan told Susan he had been passing his family's home when he saw a man attacking his wife and ran in to help, but that he had slipped in a pool of blood and the man had escaped. Then he said his wife had accused him of being behind the attack. He asked Susan for some sleeping pills and Susan gave him some Valium. Lucan then drank whisky and wrote two letters to his brother-in-law, prominent amateur jockey William Shand Kydd. Penned just hours after the murder one letter deals with financial matters. In the other letter, Lucan attempted to deny his involvement in the murder: "The most ghastly circumstances arose last night, which I have described briefly to my mother, when I interrupted the fight in Lower Belgrave Street and the man left. V accused me of having hired him. I took her upstairs and sent Frances to bed and tried to clean her up. I went into the bathroom and she left the house. The circumstantial evidence against me is strong, in that V will say it was all my doing and I will lie doggo for a while, but I am only concerned about the children. V has demonstrated her hatred for me and would do anything to see me accused."

At 1.15am, Lord Lucan left the Uckfield house in the Corsair, which was later found abandoned by police near the harbour at Newhaven in Sussex. The car's interior was stained with blood and in the boot was a piece of lead piping almost identical to the one used as the murder weapon, but slightly longer. After police found the car, they issued two warrants for Lucan's arrest and flashed a red alert to Interpol, giving police all over the world the authority to arrest him on sight. The owner of the car, Lucan's friend Michael Stoop, also received a letter from Lucan denying his involvement in the murder. Police discovered the letter was written using the same notepad discovered in the car.

Lord Lucan was never seen again. He faced social disgrace and a criminal trial. If found guilty, he faced a certain prison sentence, which he could not contemplate as he revealed in his letter to the Shand Kydds. "I am only concerned about the children," he wrote. "For them to go through life knowing their father had been in the dock accused of attempted murder would be too much for them."

After Lord Lucan vanished, his children were initially raised by their mother Lady Lucan. However, in 1982, she had a mental breakdown and lost custody. The children went to live with Lady Lucan's sister Christina and her husband William Shand Kydd. Lady Lucan did not contest this. She and her children are no longer on speaking terms. Lady Lucan said she "became involuntarily addicted to benzodiazepines"; she was admitted to Banstead Hospital in December 1983, where she stayed for seven months. Since 1987, Lady Lucan has publicly stated that her husband is not alive and she sometimes uses the prefix "dowager" to make her position as a widow clear.

Friends and family of Lord Lucan have said that after the murder, he probably jumped from a ferry or off cliffs. In his absence, he was found guilty of Rivett's murder by a coroner's jury on 19th June 1975; he was the last person in Britain to be convicted at an inquest. In October 1999, Lord Lucan was declared legally dead. In 2005, Scotland Yard issued Lord Lucan's family with an affidavit, confirming they stopped looking for him six months after he disappeared.

Over the years, there have been rumours that Lord Lucan fled the country and lived as a fugitive. There have been false sightings of the earl in France, Sicily, Colombia, India, Canada, Botswana, Australia and New Zealand. Many people suggested he was in South Africa. At the time of his disappearance, Africa was the perfect place for someone to vanish. Its isolated estates run by wealthy white farmers – many with connections to the English aristocracy – made ideal hiding places. In October 2004, the theories gathered popularity after a "cold case review" of Rivett's murder was ordered using DNA profiling.

Claims Lord Lucan fled to Africa were strengthened in February 2012, when a woman said she helped him see two of his three children, George and Frances, in the 1970s and 1980s by arranging for them to fly to Africa. The woman – referred to as Jill Findlay, although that was not her real name – worked as a secretary for Lord Lucan's millionaire friend John Aspinall. She said the disgraced earl viewed the children from a distance without their knowledge, recalled that the children went to the Treetops Hotel in Kenya and believed they flew on to Gabon. The woman also claimed she was invited to meetings where Lord Lucan was discussed by her boss and the business tycoon Sir James Goldsmith. She said: "Instructions were to make arrangements for Lord Lucan to see his children and to do that I had to book his two eldest children on flights to Africa. It was between 1979 and 1981. It was in Gabon, from what I understand, that their father would observe them, which is what he wanted to do. Just to see how they were growing up and look at them from a distance."

Other sources also insisted that George and Frances met their father during the visits to Africa. One investigator claimed he discovered bar and room receipts from a Namibia hotel in their names from as recently as 2000. It added weight to the belief that Lord Lucan was alive in 2000. Lord Lucan's brother, Hugh Bingham, said he was "sure" the aristocrat made good his escape and started a new life for himself after the brutal killing. When asked if he thought his brother had fled to Africa, he declared: "I am sure he did, yes. But what connection there is I don't know."

From the beginning, detectives hunting Lord Lucan believed he had been spirited away by his privileged friends. Almost every senior police officer connected with the case believed Lord Lucan lived in secret in Africa – including the original investigating officer, Detective Chief Superintendent Roy Ranson. He visited Africa several times and spoke to people who were convinced the fugitive aristocrat was hiding there. The detective spent most of his career searching for the elusive peer, continuing even after he retired from the Metropolitan Police; he kept a photograph of Lord Lucan in his wallet until the day he died.

Detective Chief Superintendent Drummond Marvin, who later took over the case, said: "I have no doubt that he got clean away with the help of his upper-crust friends – the Sloane Square Mafia, who I believe still help him to this day. A lot of people think Lucan killed himself by jumping into the Channel but I don't think so. In my experience you have to be bloody brave or completely mad to commit suicide and we know he wasn't brave or mad. I believe he is in Africa. I have information that he is there and using his British contacts to pour badly needed investments and hard currency into their coffers."

Some suspected that Lord Lucan's friends and fellow members at the Clermont Club, Sir James Goldsmith and John Aspinall, had helped him to vanish. The pair, both now dead, had had access to light aircraft and links to Africa. Aspinall admitted shortly after the disappearance he would have helped Lord Lucan "whatever the consequences". A BBC documentary claimed that George and Frances were secretly flown to Africa with the help of safari-park owner Aspinall so their father could see them. Private investigator Ian Crosby extensively researched the Lord Lucan mystery and believed Namibia held the key to how the earl vanished. The country had no diplomatic relations with the UK at the time of his disappearance, in common with several other nearby states, and it would have been easy for the peer to move around without fear of capture. Crosby claimed he had new evidence in the form of hotel and telephone records.

Lord Lucan doted on his children. If, as Lord Lucan's brother said, he escaped to Africa he would have found it hard to have no further contact with them. His three children and his wife have always maintained the belief that Lucan drowned in the English Channel. Lady Lucan reiterated her view when Jill Findlay's claims came to light, dismissing them as nonsense. Lady Lucan told the *Daily Mirror*: "It does not make sense. He died soon after the murder. It's rubbish, I can guarantee they didn't go to Africa. It's ridiculous, it's false. The children were wards of court, at boarding school. I was their carer. I would have known if they had gone to Africa. I had to get permission from the court to take them abroad or even into the country. I never took them abroad. It's boring to say he went abroad. He's not the sort of Englishman to cope abroad. He likes England, he couldn't speak foreign languages and preferred English food … It's so obvious he's dead. It was nearly forty years ago, he would be seventy-six now. And why would he only want to see two of the children, not all three? They have forgotten about Camilla. He would want to see all three children … I say he parked his car, had a sleep then when he woke up his resolve hardened. He then drove to Newhaven in East Sussex, dumped the car and the police found it there. By 8th November he was dead. He jumped off a ferry."

Soon after the claims hit the press, Lord Lucan's son George spoke for the first time about his father's disappearance. He wrote to the *Daily Mirror*: "I have not, to the best of my knowledge, seen my father since November 1974."

George admitted spending time in Namibia and South Africa over the previous 20 years but denied travelling to Gabon. He said in his email: "I've never been to Gabon, although I have spent time in Namibia and South Africa recuperating from a decade of coffee-swilling investment banking. I also, as an Arabic speaker, spend a lot of time in North Africa, where I keep a yacht. My father was declared dead by a High Court judge over a decade ago. I have a sworn affidavit from the Metropolitan Police and every member of my family, mother excepted, attesting to their belief that my father is dead. To suggest that I have met and spoken with my father is to make me a possible accessory to a grisly murder. It is to call me a criminal."

His "best guess" was that his gambler father had hired someone to burgle the house as part of an insurance fraud. George said that the letters written on the day of the murder by his father were "suicide notes". He told the *Daily Mirror*: "I've never thought dad was still alive. But if he were, the last place he'd be is in a 99% black African country, hanging out in a three-piece suit. It would make it very easy to find him. If he had gone anywhere – which I don't believe he did – he would have gone to somewhere like Austria or Germany."

Nevertheless, the rumours that Lord Lucan was in Africa refused to die. In December 2012, BBC's *Inside Out* programme claimed that detectives were given intelligence that Lord Lucan was alive and secretly living in Mozambique as recently as 2002. Photographs of a man using the name John Crawford passed to Scotland Yard by an unknown source were said to be so good they could be compared to the missing peer using facial-recognition software. BBC journalist Glenn Campbell travelled to South Africa to meet Lord Lucan's brother, Hugh Bingham, for the programme. Hugh said: "I believe my brother was innocent but I don't believe he would commit suicide. He was a man of considerable resourcefulness, so I imagine he used those resources to remove himself from the picture."

But Hugh dismissed the Mozambique link, saying he doubted his brother would have settled there. The BBC documentary revealed another Lord Lucan lead from 1979, when he was allegedly seen in Scotland. A mystery tipster told detectives that Lord Lucan was a regular visitor to a large retreat owned by a close friend. Former Flying Squad detective Tony Russell revealed he was told to pose as a writer and rent a cottage on the same estate for a year with a female police constable. But the retired officer said he never got the go-ahead to begin the operation and is unsure if it took place.

Inside Out made a further revelation that a mystery man may have been living in the house in London, where Rivett was beaten to death. It said he may have been the boyfriend of one of the women in the property at the time Rivett was killed. BBC researchers found a statement, made by the peer's sister-in-law Lady Sarah Gibbs, which they say was not shown at Rivett's inquest. Gibbs said Lord Lucan's daughter Camilla, then aged four, told her about a man living at the house, which her mother shared with her brother George and sister Frances. Camilla suggested he could have been a boyfriend of her mother – but Lady Sarah is believed to have said he was in a relationship with Rivett.

In February 2013, it emerged Lord Lucan may have fled to a remote Scottish island as detectives hunted him. According to a police report seen by Rivett's son, Neil Berriman, the earl hid near the ruins of a monastery on the tiny island of Eigg, 10 miles off the west coast of Scotland. The internal Scotland Yard document from 1979 is said to reveal the fact that police were so confident the peer had visited Eigg they even considered sending a detective to live there undercover.

A builder from Liphook in Hampshire, Berriman told the *Daily Mirror* he had recently been shown a copy of the report and that an entire page of the document was devoted to Lord Lucan's suspected Scottish hideaway. He said it stated police believed the peer had visited the island more than once, staying near the ruins of Kildonan monastery on its east coast.

They believed that Lord Lucan, who was a keen sailor and powerboat racer, may have used a large seagoing vessel, which was moored off the coast, to travel to and from Eigg and to sail further afield. Berriman said: "The document I have seen was an internal review of the investigation, a summary of the information gathered and what needed to be followed up. It said they believed Lord Lucan had used a property on Eigg as a possible bolthole and had visited it more than once. It mentioned a commercial, or some kind of powered vessel, which detectives believed he used to get to the island from the Scottish mainland. Scotland Yard was sufficiently convinced by this intelligence that they considered sending an inspector named Tony Russell to the island to pose as a writer, to essentially spy on the building."

Berriman's claims came just two months after *Inside Out* revealed that Detective Chief Inspector David Gerring, who originally investigated Rivett's murder and died in 2004, believed Lucan had fled to Scotland. It reported Gerring left diaries and notes saying Lord Lucan had visited "an estate" in the Scottish Highlands in the 1970s. Berriman, who was only seven when Rivett was murdered, only discovered she was his birth mother after his adoptive mother died in 2004. He added: "It doesn't matter how many years have passed since my mother's death. I am determined to seek justice for her."

Detectives, investigative journalists and amateur sleuths have circled the globe trying to find Lord Lucan. A lot of elderly, eccentric Englishmen in out-of-the-way places have had the finger pointed at them – all incorrectly. If Lucan had survived, he could not live in isolation. Anyone who found the disgraced peer would become a millionaire overnight from book and film deals, so the temptation to turn him in would be irresistible. Despite ongoing press interest and a massive police investigation, there has been no verified sighting of Lord Lucan since 1974. The crime has become one of the most famous murder mysteries of all time. Scotland Yard has never closed the inquiry into the murder of Rivett. The case is still open and officers review it periodically. If the disgraced peer did elude the authorities for decades he must have had the skills of the fictional character he was once asked to play on screen: James Bond.

Another notorious figure who has gone down in British history is Czech-born British millionaire Robert Maxwell. An archetypal larger-than-life figure and modern-day Citizen Kane, his was a story of rags to riches. He was born Ján Ludvík Hyman Binyamin Hoch into a poor Jewish family in 1923, in what was then Czechoslovakia. During the Second World War, he joined the Czechoslovak army in exile and later fought in the British army, winning the Military Cross. Most of his family died in the Holocaust. Maxwell gained British citizenship in 1946 and went on to become a Labour member of parliament, a publisher, football-club owner, newspaper proprietor and world statesman. It was only after his mysterious death at sea off the Canary Islands in 1991 that the magnate's debts and dubious ways of doing business became known.

Maxwell had a flamboyant lifestyle. He lived in Headington Hill Hall, a luxurious mansion in Oxford, flew around in a helicopter and sailed in one of the world's biggest yachts, *Lady Ghislaine*. Maxwell was also vain, keeping a personal hairdresser on 24-hour standby to dye any white hairs. The 68-year-old tycoon had his locks and eyebrows dyed every two weeks – but if a rogue white hair dared to appear while he was abroad, his hairdresser flew to his aid with a container of L'Oreal Crescendo. Maxwell was on first-name terms with Eastern European leaders, including Russian President Mikhail Gorbachev, and regarded men like Israeli Premier Yitzhak Shamir and German Chancellor Helmut Kohl as friends. Speaking to Nelson Mandela after he was freed in South Africa, Maxwell boasted: "I've negotiated with every American president since Eisenhower and every Soviet leader since Stalin."

Admired, revered and feared during his lifetime, Maxwell's enemies called him the "Bouncing Czech". A litigious man with a large ego, he used his significant funds and considerable power to protect his reputation. Satirical magazine *Private Eye* nicknamed the entrepreneur "Cap'n Bob" and was at the receiving end of various libel actions taken out by him. Maxwell hoodwinked everyone: presidents and prime ministers, royals, lords and ladies were taken in by the man in the electric blue suit, until the discovery of his body floating in the Atlantic Ocean after he fell – or threw himself – from his yacht signalled the need to turn their heads in the opposite direction.

Maxwell died on 5th November 1991. His body was found in the Atlantic off the Canary Islands after he disappeared from his yacht, *Lady Ghislaine*, during a holiday cruise between Tenerife and Las Palmas. Maxwell, the only passenger on board, had joined the *Lady Ghislaine* in Gibraltar for a few days rest. The sea was calm and weather conditions were good. Skipper Gus Rankin said he was "mystified" as to how Maxwell could have fallen overboard. At 8.30pm on 4th November, Maxwell went ashore at Santa Cruz in Tenerife to have dinner alone in a restaurant. He returned to the ship at 10pm and the *Lady Ghislaine* set sail. Captain Rankin said: "Mr Maxwell wanted to cruise all night out at sea and we decided to head in the direction of Gran Canaria."

The tycoon was last seen by the crew strolling on deck at 4.25am. His last message was a telephone call to the bridge at 4.45am, asking them to turn down the air conditioning. From then on, his last hours remain a mystery. The round trip ended when the yacht dropped anchor again five miles off the southern end of Tenerife at 9.30am. It was not for another 90 minutes that the crew realized something was amiss. Captain Rankin said: "Mr Maxwell was up until the early hours of the morning, so we naturally assumed he was having a good lie-in. Unusually, the telephone didn't ring until 11am. The phone is usually ringing off the hook by 8am even when Mr Maxwell is on vacation."

The 11am call was put through to Maxwell's stateroom. There was no answer. Captain Rankin went to Maxwell's quarters. There was no sign of him. The crew searched the yacht three times. There was still no sign of him. At 12.15pm, the captain sent a distress satellite: "Man overboard." A huge air-and-sea search ensued and, at 6pm, when the search was about to end for the night, news came that a body had been found. It was Maxwell.

Maxwell's death stunned the heads of big business and politics. Tributes flooded in from all over the world. Papers talked of the courage, daring, fearlessness, restless energy, humour – and bullying – of the tycoon who came from nowhere. Press reports portrayed a man of power, which he wielded ruthlessly, and a man of kindness, which he distributed generously. He emerged as part monster, part magic. The media was rife with speculation about Maxwell's death, simply because no one saw it happen. There was no evidence of water in his lungs. The Spanish authorities issued a death certificate stating cardiorespiratory arrest. One theory was that a pulmonary seizure caused the heart attack. While the world waited for a complete autopsy report, all sorts of theories regarding Maxwell's death emerged – from murder to suicide. No one who knew him well believed that he killed himself. The autopsy revealed that Maxwell died of natural causes. He probably died of a massive heart attack before he toppled into the sea.

On 10th November, Maxwell was laid to rest in Jerusalem, in Israel's most sacred cemetery. In a moving sunset ceremony near the top of the Mount of Olives, he was mourned with the kind of tributes usually reserved for political leaders. Saluting the tycoon before the burial, Israeli President Chaim Herzog said: "He scaled the heights. Kings and barons besieged his doorstep. Many admired him. Many disliked him. But nobody remained indifferent to him."

Herzog was joined by Israel's Prime Minister Yitzhak Shamir, cabinet ministers Ariel Sharon, Moshe Arens and Ehud Olmert, along with leader of the opposition and family friend, Shimon Peres. Herzog, a wartime friend of Maxwell, said: "We have gathered to lament the tragic and untimely passing of a mighty man, a man of courage, vision and daring enterprise, a man cast in a heroic mould. It is right and proper that he be here at last among us. I would have no doubt but that his last wish would have been that those in his family will carry the torch that he bore and continue to maintain the tradition of involvement in Israel."

Some 300 mourners packed Israel's Hall of Nations. Among them were Maxwell's wife, Betty, and their children. Dignitaries in attendance included Shadow Foreign Secretary and former *Daily Mirror* journalist Gerald Kaufman, former Archbishop of Canterbury Lord Coggan and Britain's ambassador to Israel, Mark Elliott.

Then came a dramatic announcement. On 3rd December, Maxwell's sons Ian and Kevin resigned from the boards of Maxwell Communication Corporation and Mirror Group Newspapers. Investigators had discovered that £526 million had vanished from Maxwell's company coffers in the weeks before the tycoon died, including £426 million from pension funds.

It became clear that of the millions gone, £350 million of it was money from the Mirror Group Newspapers pension fund. On 4th December 1991, the *Daily Mirror* reacted with a front page baldly stating the facts: "Millions Missing From the *Mirror*". Accompanying the headline was an editorial promising the paper would investigate the fraud – "warts and all". Maxwell had taken over the Mirror Group in 1984 and his arrival heralded a turbulent period for the *Daily Mirror*. It was not long before the paper was plunged into controversy. In 1990, a BBC *Panorama* programme revealed that, at Maxwell's insistence, a spot-the-ball competition in the paper had been rigged by placing the ball in a position so no reader could win, to avoid paying out £1 million.

Detectives from the Serious Fraud Squad moved in to probe the mystery of the missing millions amid dark tales of secret midnight meetings called to shift fortunes from place to place. It emerged that, when Maxwell died, he was coming under increasing pressure to meet massive debts incurred by his private companies. Most of the money had disappeared in September and October from the pension funds of three firms: Mirror Group Newspapers, Maxwell Communication Corporation and market research company AGB. A further £100 million went missing from Mirror Group accounts – half of it in the last few days before Maxwell died. Clandestine late-night meetings succeeded in moving many millions – and involved few authorizing signatures. Maxwell had been secretly diverting millions of pounds from two of his companies and from employee pension funds in an effort to keep solvent.

On 6th December, the *Daily Mirror* revealed that Maxwell had been challenged about the missing Mirror Group millions just before his death. He responded with a terrible lie. Finance director Lawrence Guest confronted Maxwell in his ninth-floor office high above Holborn Circus in London. He asked about £47 million which had vanished from the newspaper group's coffers, and said he was so worried about it he was unable to sleep. Maxwell told him: "Don't worry. You are losing sleep and that's not right."

Then Maxwell paused and added: "You will receive everything. Don't worry."

The confrontation happened on 21st October, 10 days before Maxwell set sail for his last voyage aboard his yacht. It was Guest's second attempt to voice concern to the publisher about the vanishing cash. Six days earlier, he questioned Maxwell during a meeting, where he was stalled. In confidential notes made after the meeting, Guest wrote: "I am now convinced that

[Mirror Group Newspapers] resources have been used to support other parts of the group. But I have no proof. I think I have frightened the chairman, but my main concern must be to get the money back. I think I am in a situation that nothing more will flow out although I don't have the machinery to stop it."

Maxwell's "don't worry" assurances were the last words he spoke to Guest about the Mirror Group's finances. The pair were due to meet again on 1st November for a meeting at which Mirror Group's chairman was also poised to ask questions. However, Maxwell left for his ill-fated boat trip the day before.

The extent of Maxwell's need to be in control became evident when the *Daily Mirror* published details of his bugging operation, around the corner from Maxwell Communication Corporation's headquarters in Holborn, which contained £30,000-worth of sophisticated equipment. In the midst of the amazing electronic display sat a video cassette that mocked the unsuspecting targets of surveillance with its ironic title: "PROTECT YOUR STAFF". The listening devices were in an eight foot by five foot room, once a stationery store, protected by a coded and alarmed entry system. There were multiple-deck tape recorders on a cascade system that triggered one tape as another ran out, six-hour and 12-hour tape recorders, and video recorders thought to have been used to play back film shot from hidden cameras. There were hidden radio bugs, sound amplifiers to listen in to even whispered conversations and a special receiver to pick up mobile phone frequencies.

Eventually, investigators discovered that when Maxwell went overboard,

£925 million went missing with him, stolen from the Mirror Group, his other companies and their pension funds. The big losers were thousands of pensioners stripped of their security and small shareholders robbed of their investments. The pensioners campaigned and a large part of the pension fund was recovered. In 1995, investment banks, accountants and what remained of Maxwell's media companies paid £276 million to the fund in an out-of-court settlement, and the British government gave a further £100 million.

In 1992, the Maxwell companies filed for bankruptcy protection. Maxwell's son Kevin was declared bankrupt with debts of £400 million. He and his brother, along with two other former directors, went on trial for conspiracy to defraud in 1995. They were acquitted. The court heard of Maxwell's power and dominance and how "the board just rubber-stamped his decision". Kevin said his father had stretched the rules over his ownership of football clubs by taking over control of one and putting him and his brother Ian in charge of others. Kevin said he was chairman of Oxford United, which was a small club and needed to sell players to survive. His father, as chairman of Derby County – later run by Ian – "would and did buy players from Oxford and the timing and prices were determined by him". He added: "The transfer of players and paying of fees are strikingly similar to the corporate transfers we have heard about in this court."

Kevin told the court his father was a bully who would "stretch the law as far as he could". He said his father "was someone who inspired a great loyalty – he was a charismatic leader. But he wasn't motivated by money. He was motivated by power – the ability to influence events and to make a difference and to change things. He was an exceedingly generous individual to people who worked for him and even those who wrote to him. If he could help, he would help."

He went on: "He was capable of being extremely charming to people, to be winning – but he was also capable of verbal brutality, public dressing downs, not only of his children but senior managers. He was capable of being a bully. In Mirror Group Newspapers there would be daily meetings of senior management, people responsible for production, distribution and editorial. If any of these managers had the misfortune to be reporting an event which displeased him, the guy would have a strip torn off him in front of everyone else. The humiliation would be in public in front of his peers and it would be total."

Kevin described his father's overbearing manner and how he would deliberately give his senior employees menial tasks to do, like opening the mail. He said: "It was part of his ritual humiliation and he would get extremely angry if they didn't handle it the way he would. It was his way of imposing control and discipline over people – putting the fear of God up them."

Maxwell's threatening ways may have cost him his life, according to a book published in 2002 by journalists Gordon Thomas and Martin Dillon: *The Assassination of Robert Maxwell: Israel's Super Spy*. They claimed that Maxwell issued one threat too many, and he threatened the Israeli secret service, Mossad. Drawing on interviews and documents, including FBI reports and secret intelligence files from behind the Iron Curtain, the authors suggested Maxwell had worked as a spy for Mossad for six years.

In that time, he had free access to Margaret Thatcher's Downing Street, to Ronald Reagan's White House, to the Kremlin and to the corridors of power throughout Europe. On top of which, he had built himself a position of power within the crime families of Eastern Europe, teaching them how to funnel their vast wealth from drugs, arms smuggling and prostitution to banks in safe havens around the globe.

Maxwell passed on all the secrets he learned to Mossad in Tel Aviv. He told his controllers who they should target and how they should do it. He appointed himself as Israel's unofficial ambassador to the Soviet bloc. Mossad saw the advantage in that. Having learned many of the key secrets of the Soviet Empire, Maxwell was given his greatest chance to be a spy. Mossad had stolen from America the most important piece of software in the American arsenal. Maxwell was given the job of marketing the stolen software, called Promis. Mossad had reconstructed the software and inserted into it a device that enabled them to track any purchaser's use of it. Sitting in Israel, Mossad would know exactly what was going on inside all the intelligence services that bought it. In all, Maxwell sold the software to 42 countries, including China and Soviet bloc nations. His greatest triumph was selling it to the very heart of America's nuclear defence system, Los Alamos.

The more successful Maxwell became the more risks he took and the more dangerous he was to Mossad. At the same time, the public side of Maxwell, who then owned 400 companies, began to unwind. He spent lavishly and lost money on deals. The more he lost, the more he tried to claw money from the banks. Then he saw a way out of his problems. He was approached by Vladimir Kryuchkov, then head of the KGB. Spymaster and tycoon met in the utmost secrecy in the Kremlin. Kryuchkov had an extraordinary proposal. He wanted Maxwell to help orchestrate the overthrow of Mikhail Gorbachev, the reformist Soviet leader. That would bring to an end a fledgling democracy and a return to the Cold War days. In return, Maxwell's massive debts would be wiped out by a grateful Kryuchkov, who planned to replace Gorbachev. The KGB chief wanted Maxwell to use the *Lady Ghislaine* as a meeting place between the Russian plotters, Mossad chiefs and Israel's top politicians. The plan was for the Israelis to go to Washington and say that democracy could not work in Russia and that it was better to allow the country to return to a modified form of Communism, which America could help to control. In return, Kryuchkov would guarantee to free hundreds of thousands of Jews and dissidents in the Soviet republics.

Kryuchkov told Maxwell that he would be seen as a saviour of all those Jews. It was a proposal Maxwell could not refuse. However, when he put it to his Mossad controllers they were horrified. They said Israel would have no part in such a madcap plan. For the first time, Maxwell had failed to get his own way. He started to threaten and bluster. He then demanded that, for past services, he should immediately receive a quick fix of £400 million to save his crumbling empire or he would expose all he had done for Mossad.

Instead of providing the money, a small group of Mossad officers set about planning Maxwell's murder. They feared that he was going to publicly expose all Mossad had done in the time he worked for them, and they knew that he was gradually becoming mentally unstable and paranoid. He was taking a cocktail of drugs – Halcion and Xanax – which had serious side effects. The group of Mossad plotters sensed Maxwell could cause incalculable harm to Israel. The plan to kill him was prepared in the utmost secrecy. A four-man squad was briefed. Then Maxwell was contacted. He was told to fly to Gibraltar, go aboard the *Lady Ghislaine* and sail to the Canary Islands. There, at sea, he would receive his £400 million quick fix in the form of a banker's draft. Maxwell did as he was told.

On the night of 4th November 1991, unknown to the *Lady Ghislaine* crew, the death squad had cast an electronic net over the yacht to block all radio transmissions. The security cameras on-board had been switched off. After midnight, there were only two men on the bridge. Maxwell appeared on deck 120 feet behind them. He had been instructed to do so in a previous message from Mossad. A small boat came alongside. On board were four black-suited men. Three scrambled on to the yacht. In a second, it was all over. Two held Maxwell. The third plunged a syringe into his neck behind his ear. A measured dose of nerve agent was injected. Maxwell was immobilized and lowered off the deck into the water. As Victor Ostrovsky, a former Mossad agent told the book authors: "On that cold night Mossad's problems with Robert Maxwell were over."

Many different theories have circulated about what really happened on board the *Lady Ghislaine*. What is without doubt is that Maxwell's fraud was the desperate action of a desperate man, striving to save an empire with debts of £3 billion. However, he was also an egomaniac, bully, fantasist, inveterate crook and, arguably, amoral. However Maxwell met his death, he died a man destroyed – both his empire and reputation were on the verge of ruin. His legacy lies in tatters and his name is disgraced.

The last fallen icon to feature in this book is also its most notorious. His crimes were many and of the most distasteful kind. As much as many want to erase his memory, to do so would be a disservice to his hundreds of victims. To remember him is a cautionary tale of how the power and wealth that accompany fame can be misused to conceal the darkest deeds. That man is DJ and TV presenter Jimmy Savile.

After the 84-year-old bachelor was found dead at his home in Leeds on 29th October 2011, he was hailed for his talent and his work for charity. The cigar-smoking, tracksuit-wearing, bling-decked Savile was a familiar figure on radio and TV from the 1960s to 1990s. He hosted BBC TV shows *Top of the Pops* and *Jim'll Fix It*, which were aimed at children and teenagers. Portrayed as a generous eccentric, he raised an estimated £40 million in funds for charities and worked as a hospital volunteer. His fundraising efforts and celebrity status opened doors to the elite. Savile mixed with the cream of society, including royalty, politicians, pop stars, top clergymen and high-ranking police officers. Within a year of his death, however, the truth about the one-time star was revealed: he was a serial child abuser. Within two years, Savile was branded Britain's most prolific sex offender.

Savile started out in the music business as a dance-hall manager in Manchester and then in Leeds. He played records and the youngsters danced. Before then, venues would just have bands on so he became the first dance hall DJ. His following in the dance halls attracted attention and Savile was signed up by Radio Luxembourg and then Radio 1. Building on his success, Savile switched to TV.

FALLEN IDOLS

The flamboyant Savile became used to accolades, including honorary degrees. In 1971, he received an Order of the British Empire for services to charity and broadcasting. In 1990, he was knighted in the Queen's Birthday Honours and received a papal knighthood. When he died, Savile was talked about in saintly terms and, as an iconic media figure, held in high regard for his charity work. But his celebrity status and charity campaigning masked a sordid truth. For more than 50 years, Savile toured the country preying on the vulnerable and weak, subjecting hundreds of innocent victims to a vile catalogue of abuse. The ghastly details of his crimes shocked the world. In Britain, a horrified nation asked how a man could commit so many terrible crimes, for so many decades, and questioned how some of its most famous institutions had managed to remain unaware of the real nature of the monster in their midst.

Savile's real nature was revealed thanks to an ITV1 documentary, *Exposure: The Other Side of Jimmy Savile*, screened in October 2012. It contained horrifying testimony from five alleged victims, who claimed Savile attempted to take advantage of them sexually while they were all under 16. One woman, named as Val, claimed Savile indecently assaulted her "dozens of times" and raped her. The documentary revealed that Savile referred to *Top of the Pops* as his "happy hunting ground" for youngsters. A former newsroom assistant at BBC Leeds said she caught Savile in his dressing room with his hand up a girl's skirt. She said: "I opened the door and Jimmy had a girl of about fourteen sat on his knee. He had his left arm up her skirt and was kissing her. It wasn't just a peck on the cheek, like she'd jumped on his knee – it was a sexual advance to this girl."

One alleged victim in the documentary, Fiona, 14 at the time, claimed she was abused after Savile visited Duncroft Approved School in Surrey and invited girls to ride in his Rolls-Royce. She said he made her perform a sex act, adding: "I thought it was expected of me."

Another student at the school, Charlotte, claimed: "I remember sitting on his lap – the next thing, I felt his hand go up my jumper and on my breast. I freaked out and started swearing. Then I was dragged off by two of his staff. I was told what a filthy mouth I had. They said, 'How can you make those terrible accusations? Uncle Jimmy does nothing but good for the school.'"

Former detective Mark Williams-Thomas, who investigated the evidence for the documentary, said: "The accounts all connected in terms of modus operandi. I had no doubt the people making the allegations were telling the truth. The great shame is that Savile is not alive to face the allegations. We are right to give these women a voice – one not heard while they were children."

Scotland Yard launched an inquiry into the allegations. The revelations in the TV documentary were just the tip of an iceberg. Hundreds of people started to come forward, claiming to have been abused by Savile. Some told their stories to the press in articles that made for grisly reading. Porters and nurses at Stoke Mandeville Hospital in Aylesbury broke their silence to say they told patients to pretend to be asleep as Savile roamed the wards at night. It was revealed that Savile had been barred from the BBC's "Children in Need" campaign over his "creepy" behaviour. There were calls for the former star to be stripped of his knighthoods even though they ended when he died. Inquiries and reviews were held by the BBC, the Department of

Health and the Crown Prosecution Service.

The media interviewed celebrities who revealed they had heard rumours about the star's sexual behaviour. ChildLine founder Esther Rantzen, who worked at the BBC alongside Savile, said: "I feel that we in television, in his world, in some way colluded with him as a child abuser – because I now believe that's what he was. We all blocked our ears to the gossip. We made him into the Jimmy Savile who was untouchable. *Jim'll Fix It* was for children – he was a sort of God-like figure. These children were powerless. The jury isn't out any more. What upsets me is that not one of these children could ask for help. The abuse of power was as great as the sexual abuse."

On 11th January 2013, the National Society for the Prevention of Cruelty to Children and the Metropolitan Police published a report, *Giving Victims a Voice*, following the investigation into claims Savile was a sexual abuser. It revealed that the DJ and TV star had targeted 450 children and adults in a campaign of sexual abuse over six decades. The report said he used a cloak of showbiz eccentricity to mask his depraved secret life, and the power of celebrity to control those he targeted in order to escape justice.

His youngest victim was an eight-year-old boy and the oldest a woman of 47. During his perverted reign he carried out 34 rapes on males and females and 126 indecent assaults. His attacks happened in 28 police force areas. He struck at the BBC where he worked, in hospitals and hospices, schools and on the road. Investigation chief, Commander Peter Spindler, said Savile had "groomed the nation". The report revealed he even molested a dying child at London's Great Ormond Street Hospital in 1971. And he was still carrying out his sick attacks at the age of 79, when he groped a schoolgirl off camera on the final episode of *Top of the Pops* in 2006. However, his terrified victims were largely ignored or not taken seriously, as it was their word against that of a household name who had millions of fans.

Detective Superintendent David Gray of the Metropolitan Police, who compiled the report with the NSPCC, said: "The sheer scale and the severity of his offending is appalling. He spent every minute of every waking day thinking about it, whenever an opportunity came along he has taken it. He is programmed to think and act in that way. He only picked the most vulnerable, the ones least likely to speak out against him."

The NSPCC director of child protection advice and awareness, Peter Watt, added: "Savile was one of the most prolific sex offenders the NSPCC has ever dealt with. He cunningly built his life around trying to gain access to children and hid in plain sight behind a veil of eccentricity. The sheer scale of Savile's abuse over six decades simply beggars belief. Every number represents a victim that will never get justice now he is dead."

The presenter even boasted to detectives who started to have suspicions about him in 2009 that he had friends in the senior ranks of West Yorkshire Police who helped him cover up allegations. Scotland Yard's Specialist Crime Investigations chief, Spindler, said the report "paints a stark picture emphasising the tragic consequences of when vulnerability and power collide".

Savile's earliest reported offence was in Manchester in 1955 when he was 29. The report said 50 offences happened on hospital or hospice premises, 33 in TV or radio studios and 14 in schools. He struck at 13

National Health Service institutions, including Wheatfield's Hospice in Leeds, where he allegedly attacked a schoolgirl visitor in 1977. Other victims were said to have been targeted at Stoke Mandeville Hospital, Leeds General Infirmary, and Broadmoor and Ashworth high-security psychiatric hospitals. Almost a fifth of his victims were boys. A total of 18 girls and 10 boys under the age of 10 were abused, as well as 23 girls and 15 boys aged 10 to 13.

The report revealed Savile sexually abused children at the BBC from 1965 to 2006; at Leeds General Infirmary, where he volunteered as a porter from 1965 to 1995; at Stoke Mandeville Hospital, where he was also a porter, from 1965 to 1988; and at Duncroft School between 1970 and 1978. Other offences were committed at his holiday cottage at Glencoe in the Highlands and in his mobile home. The two most prolific years of his offending were 1975 and 1976, with 15 offences committed in each year. He reached his "peak offending period" between 1966 and 1976.

The report included examples of the way Savile targeted his victims. In 1960, a boy of 10 was seriously sexually assaulted in a hotel reception after he asked Savile for an autograph. In 1972, during a recording of *Top of the Pops*, a 12-year-old boy and two female pals were groped during a break in filming. In 2009, a 43-year-old woman was talking to Savile on a train between Leeds and London when Savile put his hand up her skirt. Savile picked children to abuse from the rejected letters of those who wrote in to his prime-time TV show, *Jim'll Fix It*, which, at its height, pulled in thousands of letters a week from youngsters hoping he would make their dreams come true. The paedophile would sift through the ones who had not been chosen and offer to pay them special visits.

Perhaps most shocking information in *Giving Victims a Voice* was that Savile had been investigated by detectives five times while still alive – by the Metropolitan Police in the 1980s and in 2003; by the Surrey force from 2007 to 2009; by Sussex Police in 2008; and by Jersey Police in 2008. None of the inquiries resulted in charges. Savile bragged to detectives he had police contacts who helped him get rid of sex abuse claims. The pervert made the boast while being quizzed under caution by Surrey Police on suspicion of sexual offences.

At the same time *Giving Victims a Voice* was published, two other reports were released. One, by the Surrey Police, looking into how the force handled three complaints, said: "He explained he has contacts within the police and whenever he receives letters alleging that he has done something wrong he gives them to contacts who 'get rid' of them." An unnamed West Yorkshire police inspector also contacted the force to confirm "that he was known to Savile and Savile gets many of these complaints". Prosecutors decided in 2009 that no case could be brought because the alleged victims would not support action. The third report, by the Crown Prosecution Service, detailed failings that prevented any case going to court. Seven alleged victims of Savile complained to police in Surrey, London, Sussex and Jersey while the disgraced presenter was alive but the CPS decided no further action should be taken.

After the allegations emerged, a memorial plaque outside Savile's former home in Scarborough, North Yorkshire, was defaced by the words "paedophile" and "rapist" being scrawled on it, before being taken down.

FALLEN IDOLS

A life-sized wooden statue of the former presenter was removed from near a children's swimming pool in Glasgow. Supermarket chain Asda stopped selling Savile fancy-dress outfits after a string of complaints. Charitable trusts using his name closed down. In Scarborough, where he was buried, signs on a clifftop path named "Savile's View" were removed. The £4,000, six feet by four feet memorial gravestone, inscribed with Savile's chilling epitaph: "It was good while it lasted", was dismantled.

Savile was a fiend in plain sight, beamed into sitting rooms nationwide. He was brazen in his abuse but, because of his celebrity, he got away with it. Skilled at manipulating those around him, he used his fame and power to prey on the most vulnerable. His iconic status dazzled those around him and they dismissed rumours as gossip. He raised money for charity – perhaps to salve his conscience, perhaps to gain access to potential victims, perhaps to create a mythical persona of himself as a decent man, perhaps all of those things. His apparent good works meant the Establishment opened its doors to him. The media that discovers stories of celebrities' drunken escapades, drug habits, misdemeanours, breakdowns and affairs failed to unearth the truth about Savile until it was too late to make him pay for his crimes. The public appeared to swallow the idea he was a loveable eccentric. A devious criminal and pervert, Savile was not brought to justice in his lifetime. The system failed. The nation has learned he was a rogue celebrity and that he may not be the only one. Rightly, his name is reviled. He is not worthy of memory – his victims are and they are surely the ultimate casualties of fame.